John G. Bennett's
Talks on
BEELZEBUB'S
TALES

John G. Bennett's
Talks on
BEELZEBUB'S
TALES

Compiled by A. G. E. Blake from
the unpublished writings and talks
of John G. Bennett

SAMUEL WEISER, INC.

York Beach, Maine

First published in 1988 by
Samuel Weiser, Inc.
Box 612
York Beach, ME 03910

Second printing, 1993

Library of Congress Cataloging-in-Publication Data

Bennett, John G. (John Godolphin), 1897-1974.
    Talks on Beelzebub's tales/John G. Bennett; compiled
by A.G.E. Blake from the unpublished writings and talks
of John G. Bennett.
        p.   cm.
    1. Gurdjieff, Georges Ivanovitch, 1872-1949. All and everything.
I. Blake, A.G.E. (Anthony George Edward) II. Title.
B4249.G84B47 1988
197'.2-dc19   88--3963
                                                CIP

ISBN 0-87728-680-9
MG

Typeset in 10 point Baskerville
Printed in the United States of America

The paper used in this publication meets the minimum requirements of the American National Standard for Permanence of Paper for Printed Library Materials Z39.48-1984.

CONTENTS

PART FIVE: *Reality*

PROLOGUE

t is past midnight. For nearly two hours, fifteen or twenty English and American pupils have been listening to a reading of a chapter from the Second Series of his writings. In another room, twenty-five or thirty members of his French group have been hearing the same chapter in French. Now we are seated round the table, as many as can crowd into the little dining room while the remainder are eating their dinner seated on the floor of the next room where the French reading was held.

Most faces are familiar, but there are two visitors from Greece whom we have not seen before, occupying places of honour on his right, and two newcomers from America who are old friends of most of those in the room. The room is very crowded, but there is no bustle of serving, for the plates have been brought in beforehand and the dishes are silently changed by those standing behind the table, who themselves are eating from the sideboard or the mantelpiece.

All attention is turned towards Gurdjieff. The meal has reached a climax for which all have been waiting. A toast has been drunk which serves as a text for a sermon which, however many times repeated, only seems to gain in its dramatic force. "Everyone must have an aim. If you have not an aim, you are not a man. I will tell you a very simple aim, **to die an honourable death**. Everyone can take this aim without any philosophising — not to perish like a dog." He then tells someone present to explain what this means, and the answer comes "Only he can die an honourable death who works on himself in life. He who does not work upon himself in life will inevitably, early, lately, perish like a dirty dog." Gurdjieff repeats that this is the first and the simplest aim which every man must set before himself, and only when he has achieved this can he go beyond it to a higher aim. As always, he suddenly turns the conversation to a joke, and in a minute the room is shaken with laughter at some story about the peculiarities of the English. But the impression remains of the overwhelming seriousness of our human situation, of the choice which confronts us between life and death.

The meal continues, and in conversation with one of the newcomers, Gurdjieff unexpectedly says, "I will tell you the first commandment of God to man. This is not one of the commandments given to Moses, which were for a special people, but one of the universal commandments which have always existed. There are many of them, perhaps twenty, but this is the first. 'Let one hand wash the other.' It is very difficult for one hand to wash itself alone, but if one hand washes the other, both will be clean." Simple words, but so spoken that they penetrate to the root of the egoism present in each one of us. We look at one another with different eyes, understanding that we are helpless alone, and realising that there is something that binds us stronger than friendship or race or creed. Even the complete strangers of half an hour since have become united with us in a common understanding.

Gurdjieff is very tired. He eats with difficulty. There is a long silence. Someone asks him a question about the publication of *Beelzebub*. He speaks of his writings, and says that they are his soldiers. With them he will make war against the old world. The old world must be destroyed in order that a new world may be born. His writings will make many friends but they will also make many enemies. When they are published, he will disappear. Perhaps he will not return. We protest that we cannot work without him. If he disappears, we will follow him. He smiles and says, "perhaps you will not find me."

The meal ends, coffee is brought. Gurdjieff sends for his favourite musical instrument, a small organ of special design, and plays a long chorale upon a Greek mode. We leave at 2:30. Three visitors returning to England in the early morning a few hours hence depart laden with gifts of food for their families.

J. G. Bennett, 1950

INTRODUCTION

he prologue was written by J.G. Bennett in 1950 to introduce a series of writings on the ideas of Mr. Gurdjieff. These circulated amongst people in Bennett's groups but were never published. The parts which specifically deal with the content of *Beelzebub's Tales* have been included in this monograph. Their origin goes back to the year before, 1949, the period just before Mr. Gurdjieff died. Bennett described it as follows.

"In 1949, Mr. Gurdjieff was living in Paris and his pupils were visiting him from all parts of the world. By far the largest contingent came from England, principally from the three groups led by Jane Heap, Kenneth Walker, and myself. I used to go as often as possible to Paris, and once a week held meetings at Denison House near Victoria Station for those who could not get to Paris. At that time, Mr. Gurdjieff spoke of coming to London and said that if he came, he expected the pupils to be familiar with *Beelzebub's Tales to His Grandson*. We therefore held weekly public readings of the book.

"I told him that many had asked me to help them to understand the difficult words and even more difficult ideas in the book. He said that I should do so as well as I could, because he would be able to say what he wanted only to people who had thoroughly studied *Beelzebub's Tales*."

In June and July of 1949, Bennett gave six lectures—just before he went to Paris for a prolonged stay three months before Gurdjieff's death. Bennett began preparing these lectures for publication as late as 1973: ". . . in spite of the development of my own understanding since they were given. At that time, I was in almost weekly contact with Gurdjieff and

very much under the influence of the many talks I had with
him about his works and his plans for the future."

The project was abandoned. Two of these lectures that we
have are not very inspiring, but their sequel in the writings of
1950 are often quite extraordinary.

"I was so deeply impressed by the extraordinary and powerful ideas of *Beelzebub's Tales* that I expected that when published they would make an instant appeal to those who
throughout the world were searching for new concepts of God,
the World and Man. In the event, the book which appeared
about a year after these lectures made little impact outside the
circle of those already interested in Gurdjieff's ideas. The book
is too hard for the ordinary reader to take, and yet its message
is for everyone."

Bennett never claimed that he was truly initiated into the
meaning of *Beelzebub's Tales*, but he often quoted Gurdjieff himself on this, saying that all real initiation is self-initiation, a
matter of understanding. This is what we have here in the part
called "Glimpses of the Truth." For twenty-five years he strug-
gled to grasp the meaning of Beelzebub and to help others
understand it. Besides the notes taken from Orage in Nott's
book *Diary of a Pupil*, there is hardly anything generally published in the way of commentary on the *Tales*. This is from one
point of view very strange, since it is undoubtedly one of the
most important books written in the past hundred years and,
according to Professor Denis Saurat who wrote to Bennett
about it many years ago, it amounts to the creation of a whole
new *mythos*, a feat only possible through an intelligence beyond
this earth. From another point of view, the task of exposition
appears too immense to undertake. Ordinary critiques such as
one that appeared in a series of articles on Gurdjieff in the
quarterly *Studies in Comparative Religion** look ridiculous and
childish. In its complexities and obscurities like an alchemical
text, in its humour and robustness like a Rabelaisian chronicle,

---

**Studies in Comparative Religion* (quarterly), "Gurdjieff in the Light of Tradi-
tion," 3 parts, 1975.

in its breadth like a monumental work of historical analysis, in its passion like a sermon and in its compassion like something almost sacramental — *Beelzebub's Tales* surpasses all ordinary points of view. It belongs to a new kind of thought — or a very ancient one — a kind that comes from the depths of our nature. It is an expression of Objective Reason.

Approaching the end of his life working at Sherborne House, Bennett gave many talks on the meaning of *Beelzebub's Tales* and luckily most of these were recorded. These talks have been incorporated into this monograph. I have included talks which are not simply interpretation, but taking the questions further: that is true interpretation. Bennett was never satisfied with explaining, but saw that each one of us has to create the meaning in ourselves by our own work.

I have been quite astonished at some of these talks, most of which I was fortunate enough to hear at the time they were given. These insights must not be lost. All who can must work to create an understanding of *Beelzebub's Tales* and take what Bennett has given us as a starting point for our own search. We need to grasp Man, the World and God quite differently. The old world is already dead. The new is to be created out of a **new vision**. Surely, that was what *Beelzebub's Tales* were for. As Gurdjieff said, his writings are his "soldiers." We must share with each other as much as we can about the "glimpses of the truth."

A. G. E. Blake, Sherborne, 1976

PART ONE

HISTORY

Glimpses of the Truth, 1974
The Arousing of Thought, 1950
The Scenario, 1949
Beelzebub as History, 1950
The Reconciling Force in History, 1950

GLIMPSES OF THE TRUTH

urdjieff's attitude to initiation was firmly stated in the earliest account of his ideas, written in 1915 and called "Glimpses of Truth."[1] This is the story of a cultured Russian and his first meeting with Gurdjieff. After Gurdjieff had given a brilliant exposition of the transformation of energies in man and the universe, making use of various diagrams, the visitor said: "This knowledge you have surprises me, why has it been hidden?" Gurdjieff explained that he could be told because he had previously worked and studied adding: "Thanks to this work, your own work, you are able to understand something of what I have told you. Let us suppose that in a year's time we should speak again on this subject, during this year you will not have waited for roast pigeon to fly into your mouth. You will have worked and your understanding will have changed. You will be more 'initiated.' You said that 'knowledge' was 'hidden.' This is not so; it is simply that people are incapable of understanding. Personally, for instance, I should be very glad if I could talk to anyone of the subjects that interest me without having to put myself on a level with their understanding and intelligence. People have too few words for the expression of certain ideas. Where it is not the words that are important but the source from which they came, in the absence of understanding it is simply impossible to speak.

"What you call 'hiding' is, in truth, the impossibility of giving what people cannot receive."

---

[1]See also *Views from the Real World* by G.I. Gurdjieff (New York: Dutton, 1975; and London: Routledge & Kegan Paul, 1974).

Gurdjieff's elaborate symbolism, uncouth neologisms and changes of terminology were not adopted to mislead and distract his followers but to ensure that they would make the effort to discover the meanings for themselves. Explanation is often a fictitious help. Initiation is real enough, but it does not consist in making things easy for the seeker.

When we have organized ideas put in front of us that our minds are able to accept, it is very hard to prevent this mind from being lazy. We say: "Now I understand" and we do not feel the need to do any work.

The truth has always been revealed to man in glimpses. It has never been unveiled because it would be impossible for man to look at it. When there is a glimpse of truth there must be something able to bear it.

Even a glimpse of the truth has an unlimited power. This is where the possibility of confusion comes in. Again and again people have seen some facet of the whole and because is has such unlimited power of attraction and understanding it is almost impossible for them to grasp that they have seen only one tiny bit. If they have power because of what has happened to them they will then convince other people that what they have seen is the whole truth.

The strange thing about this is that they are right. The truth is a whole in every one of its facets. If we have seen even one tiny part, we have seen the whole. It is only when we come to express what we have seen that the difficulty begins.

The fairy tale of the djinn and the palace illustrates our real position in front of the truth. In the *Arabian Nights* there is a story like this where some supernatural power, or djinn, builds a resplendent place opposite the palace of a king. The king is overcome by the beauty of it. The story continues to the point at which the djinn challenges the king to finish what he has built. What is left to complete is only one small window, but all of the king's resources and all the labour of his artisans do not suffice for it.

This story represents a lesson that we have to learn. The great whole is there put in front of us but something is left out. We are invited to complete it.

It will take all of our riches and everything we can do. Then we shall come to acknowledge our impotence and realize that the whole can only be completed by the whole. At the same time we have to accept the challenge.

THE AROUSING OF THOUGHT

urdjieff's methods are directly opposed to all our comfortable habits. He was concerned to bring people to understand for themselves and with this aim always before him, he never made anything easy or tried to convince anyone of anything. On the contrary, he made the approach to his ideas difficult, both intellectually and emotionally. However hard in itself a theme might be to understand, he would always make it harder by incompleteness of exposition, by introducing inner contradictions and even absurdities, and by breaking off the study as soon as comprehension had begun to dawn and not returning to it perhaps for months or even years.

Beelzebub explains to his grandson why he has adopted a particular form and sequence for his explanations about the life of man on earth. In this passage, Gurdjieff throws light on his own method of exposition, namely the intentional arousing in the student of an inner conflict of affirmation and negation, without which real understanding cannot arise. Gurdjieff's dialectic penetrates more deeply than the mind. He is not satisfied with the intellectual thesis and antithesis but understands very well what William James half says, that feeling is prior to thought.

Because Gurdjieff's dialectic is the foundation of his teaching, I have taken for the theme of this chapter the title of the first chapter of *All and Everything*. I have said that Gurdjieff called the chapter Purgatory the 'heart' of his writings, but he gave more time and care to the composition of "The Arousing of Thought" than to anything else that he wrote. His translators assert that it was completely rewritten at least seven times, and read in his presence innumerable times to old and new pupils and friends, to chance acquaintances and even to complete strangers. Gurdjieff could be in no doubt about the hostility it would provoke; offending, as it does, every canon of literary and personal taste and conveying the impression, as an eminent writer once remarked to me, of "puerile vanity verging on paranoia."

Now there are two things about Gurdjieff that no one who had any degree of close contact with him could possibly doubt, first that he had a consummate knowledge of human beings and knew exactly the reactions that would be provoked by any type of stimulus. Secondly he was more completely without vanity than anyone we have known. Although he could play to perfection any role he chose, including that of vainglorious bombast, he was inwardly so humble that it astonished him that people should wish to serve him and bring him gifts. No one who worked closely with him could doubt that he possessed powers quite unknown to ordinary man; this is attested in the sober and objective account which Ouspensky gives of his own experience.[2] Yet he used his powers with the utmost restraint and never for his own personal benefit. Above all, they were never used for purposes of show or to increase his influence over people.

I find it necessary to state and emphasize these facts because few people without previous preparation can be expected to catch the subtleties of "The Arousing of Thought." I am not sure that I am fulfilling Gurdjieff's wishes in seeking to make easier the approach to this chapter. This is not the work of an amateur first trying his hand at literary composition, or of a man whose judgment is clouded by a recent nearly fatal accident. It is written as, after long deliberation, he wished it to be written. In subsequent revision he did nothing to tone down its acerbities, but rather made any changes in the direction of increasing the antagonism it would provoke in the reader.

---

[2]Ouspensky, *In Search of the Miraculous*, Chap. XIII, p. 260 (San Diego, Calif.: Harcourt, Brace, Jovanovich, 1965; and London: Routledge & Kegan Paul, 1950).

"The Arousing of Thought" is not an isolated phenomenon, but a characteristic specimen of Gurdjieff's teaching; whether in his writing or in his personal contact with pupils. It derives from his fundamental concept of human destiny. If man is to serve the high purpose for which he was created, he must above all be free. For Gurdjieff, the greatest tragedy of modern man is his inner slavery, which is ten thousand times worse than outer slavery. Suggestibility to the written or spoken word, the readiness, as he puts it, "to believe any old tale," destroys the possibility of a normal sane existence on the earth. They are still more fatal to the prospect of attaining objective reason. Suggestibility cannot be cured by suggestion, and therefore it is necessary to touch a man at a point where he is not suggestible and plant at that point something which can grow. The issue before the man who begins reading "The Arousing of Thought" is not "Shall I accept or not what is written here?" but, "Shall I read it and try to understand something?" There is a conflict, but not an intellectual affirmation and denial. There is a struggle, but not of faith against disbelief. What then is involved? The decision whether or not to try something new. As I begin reading I become aware that Gurdjieff does not look at the world or man, himself included, from the standpoint I have been trained to adopt as reasonable, useful and right. Gurdjieff does not, like some French existentialist, regard the consciously absurd as an abstract principle. He makes of it a practical weapon for attacking the unconciously absurd. He brings into it, however, that subtlety which makes dead words into living experience.

Man is a three-brained being, and understanding does not depend upon his thoughts and feelings alone, but also upon his senses. Where the thoughts and feelings are helpless, the senses can perhaps respond. Gurdjieff therefore helps the reader to transfer himself to the new standpoint by vivid sensory images. The seven-shooted tooth with its seven drops of blood is the symbol of the unexpected rather than the unknown, and the barber dentist is the best available source of knowledge. The story of the tooth with its wild absurdities represents more exactly than any reasoned analysis or emotional rhetoric, the situation of the man who has seen that nothing makes sense and that he must follow every thread, however slender, which gives a hope of a way out of the labyrinth. Gurdjieff gives no explanation of the symbolism and the reader may not suspect it, but he undergoes a certain experience as he reads. Having watched the reaction of hundreds of people to this story, I have seen how often it leaves an impression which they are unable to forget. Nothing is suggested to them. Nothing is even explained to them, but without realising it, they begin to think in a new way. So it is throughout Gurdjieff's readings. I have heard that one of his pupils and closest friends, the late A.R. Orage, once said "Gurdjieff has buried a bone in his writings. We are like dogs who have the smell of the bone but cannot find it. If we are hungry enough, we shall go on scratching until we find the bone. And when we find the bone, we shall no longer be dogs, but men."

This is the first secret of Gurdjieff's teaching—it places obstacles at those points where the next step forward can only be made by means of an effort dictated by one's own decision. This applies to the study of his own writings as much as to the more personal methods of work.

People who know something of Zen Buddhism often remark upon the similarity of Gurdjieff's methods to those of Zen. I have no acquaintance with Zen except through the essays of Suzuki and translations of some of the Sutras. There is an apparent similarity between "The Arousing of Thought" and what Suzuki calls the Koan Exercise. The Zen master confronts his pupil with a situation either verbal or physical in which he can see no meaning. The master teaches nothing and he explains nothing. The pupil must persevere, if necessary for years, until some inner resistance breaks down and he enters the state called Satori. Satori can have different degrees but it is always the object of striving and not the way. The task Gurdjieff sets himself in "The Arousing of Thought" is to bring people to the starting point and not to the end of the journey. His methods in later stages of work with his pupils differ from anything that Suzuki describes. Suzuki, for example, writes of the schools of Nembutsu, that is, repetition. The difference seems to be in the predominance of the spirit of enquiry in the followers of Koan and the predominance of persistence and determination in those who use Nembutsu. Certainly both these qualities are demanded by Gurdjieff, but he placed understanding in advance of either, and often quoted the advice, "The benefit of an effort is proportional to the understanding with which it is performed. Until one understands what one is doing, it is better to do nothing." It seems to me that this represents a radical distinction from Zen although I have no doubt that things are very different when seen from "inside." The failure of language has seldom been more apparent than in Western attempts to understand Buddhism in any of its forms.

In "The Arousing of Thought," Gurdjieff treats the inadequacy of language and the loss of contact with reality which comes from the use of words without determined effort to give and retain for them a concrete meaning. He refers to this in the final chapter of *All and Everything* and makes it again the main theme of the Introduction to the *Second Series* of his writings. The first defence against suggestibility is to train our minds to look for concrete meanings behind words and phrases. We then see that nearly everything by which the world lives today, all the so-called ideologies, all creeds, all plans and programmes for the future, are empty, for they can change nothing in the life of man. Or, if I ask myself what is the aim of my life, the goal, if any, towards which I am striving, I see that I begin to use words which I do not understand and realise with dismay that there is no firm ground on which I can place my feet. This is the first consequence of the arousing of thought.

Gurdjieff develops, as it were casually, out of this idea in his "principle of the stick with two ends," the doctrine that every cause must produce opposite effects. In particular, that which produces satisfaction must also produce suffering and that which produces suffering must also produce satisfaction. This principle afterwards becomes one of the main themes of the book in the concept of *Parktdolg-duty or Conscious Labour and Intentional Suffering*, as the sole means by which the individuality and freedom latent in a man can become actual.

He then tells the tale of the Transcaucasian Kurd, who, having bought with his precious farthings a red pepper, feels compelled to eat it in spite of his distress, and in spite of the mockery of the passers-by. From this story comes the title sometimes given to the first chapter, "The Warning." If you embark on this way, you must engage yourself. Without engagement there will be no persistence. Reluctance to become engaged is a characteristic of human weakness. It is fear of the unknown, of discomfort and sacrifice. "No man, having put his hand to the plow, and looking back, is fit for the Kingdom of God."

After the "Warning," Gurdjieff passes to the three tales which illustrate the main aspects of "The Arousing of Thought." The first is the rejection of suggestibility, the refusal to rely upon the opinions or slavishly to imitate the behaviour of others. It is expressed in the words of his grandmother, "Either do nothing — just go to school, or do something nobody else does." This theme again is developed in the *Tales of Beelzebub*, where human suggestibility is exhibited as one of the principal causes of the unhappy situation of mankind.

Gurdjieff carried the principle into effect throughout his own life, and also in his teaching. In the story of his grandmother, he not only states the principle, but indicates that it must be put into effect through action and not through thought, I cannot be free so long as I imitate other people, above all, if I imitate them unconsciously. It was the very essence of Gurdjieff's teaching that the pupil must stand on his own feet and he took every measure, sometimes apparently harsh and brutal, to break down any tendency towards dependence upon himself. He would go to the length of depriving himself of much-needed helpers in his work rather than allow a relationship of dependence, or subordination.

At the same time, he took for granted that a teacher is necessary and made it clear why this is so. No man can work alone until he knows himself, and no one can know himself until he can be separate from his own egoism. The teacher is always needed to apply the knife, to sever the true from the false, but he can never work for his pupil, nor understand for him, nor be for him. We must work, and understand, and be, for ourselves.

The failure to make these distinctions has led to two kinds of mistakes about the role of schools and teachers. The first and obvious mistake is to exchange dependence upon the external world for dependence upon the teacher. This does not eradicate suggestibility but transfers it to every word and gesture of the teacher. Such schools are well known, and their dangers and limitations are obvious. But it is also wrong to go to the other extreme, and reject the relationship of pupil and teacher altogether, as has been done, for example, by Krishnamurti in his reaction against the tendencies of the first kind. For many years, Krishnamurti has lectured to audiences in many countries, and spoken to innumerable individuals privately upon the theme of self-sufficiency. "The truth cannot be taught — there is no hope in gurus but only in yourself." He sees mankind as slaves to everything external. This slavery is not only towards base things but to noble ideas and also to the gurus who teach them. He thus makes into an objective principle what is only the observation of a defect in those who are seeking to teach. He is entirely right in denouncing slavish dependence upon a teacher, but does not take into account the fact that the genuine teacher will take every measure to destroy such dependence. He denounces slavery to an idea, but does not realise that an idea is valid precisely to the extent that it does not lead to slavery. He himself has an Idea, namely that transformation is a process with neither past nor future, existing only here and now, in the present moment of seeing and acting. He teaches this — although it is an idea — because he does not see in it the danger of slavery. The danger exists, however, for no man can see with his own unaided vision. He must stand apart from the whole situation and see himself and the world through the eyes of objective reason. Until he has acquired such eyes, he must beg or borrow them from another.

And so we come to Gurdjieff's second principle, exemplified in the story of the tooth. There must be the spirit of enquiry. There must be in us an inner determination to understand and a refusal to put aside any awkward fact which disturbs our preconceived ideas. This is one of the banes of our scientific age. We confine our enquiries to what is respectable and fashionable. Even philosophers approach with reluctance any suggestion that they must take into account facts outside of what is traditionally accepted. One of the wisest of modern philosophers, the late Professor Whitehead, said that "The greatest danger to philosophy is narrowness in the selection of evidence."[3]

Philosophy tends to be over impressed with the success of natural science, and too acutely conscious of its own failures in the past to give any answer at all to the ultimate question, in particular, Gurdjieff's question, "What is the significance and purpose of human existence?" The result is that even philosophers — whose business it should be — virtually abandoned the search for ultimate reality and confined themselves to the interpretation of sense experience.

And so we come back to the story of Gurdijeff's tooth. It symbolises respect for irrelevant or rather, the refusal to regard as irrelevant anything which enters into human experience. It was Gurdjieff's extraordinary determination in applying the rule that nothing can be irrelevant in the search for ultimate explanations that led him finally to such a profound understanding of the sense and meaning of all existence. The very title of his book, *All and Everything*, is an expression of the principle that everything is relevant and the only knowledge worth having is the knowledge of all. He carried this principle into effect in all that he taught. When surrounded by a handful of his pupils, he would make use of the most trivial incident to demonstrate the laws which govern the whole human situation. He would never think for his pupils. They had to think for themselves, but he would often confront them with situations from which there was no escape except by a supreme effort to understand. People were often disappointed and even angry because he would never explain. In listening to him, I was often reminded of Blake's couplet,

---

[3]A.N. Whitehead, *Process and Reality* p. 477.

Everything that lives has meaning
And needs neither suckling nor weaning.

He would never add anything to a fact nor divorce it from its
context. He never stopped thinking to the end of his life. In one
of his last conversations, he referred to a former teacher of his,
who, he said, was nearly a hundred years old, and although he
had been seriously ill, had recently returned to his investiga-
tions, and was at present occupied in trying to answer the
question, "Why did God make the louse and the tiger?" This is
typical of his guiding principle that everything in the universe
has a function, and that this function can be understood in
relation to a greater whole, into whose life it enters. A louse
was for him not a freak of nature, but a significant fact in the
universe which could not be understood unless the role of even
apparently destructive and wasteful agencies could be
discovered.

Gurdjieff made a distinction between subjective and
objective science. The former which comprises all the science
we know is subjective in the sense that the scientist brings his
own meaning into his observations. He is concerned with classification and description, and with the discovery of processes
which result from such classification and description. Objective
science starts with the fundamental assumption that the universe itself is pervaded with meaning, and that this meaning
itself can be discovered. Subjective science carried to its logical
conclusion denies meaning in the universe and finds it only in
human experience. This position is in fact adopted and
defended by many scientists and philosophers at the present
time. It is not the universe, but my own existence which lacks
meaning so long as I remain with my essential nature undevel-
oped. Then to seek meaning in my own experience is to start at
the wrong end. What I shall find in my own experience is that I
do not exist as a significant individual. From this realization, I
can embark on the task of acquiring a meaning. Moreover my
meaning will not be my private concern — it will be a measure
of the part I can play in the universal drama. Such a doctrine is
bound to be a stumbling block to the "orthodox" scientists of

our generation, who have been brought up to reject the idea that such things as objective "ends" and universal "meanings" are illusory. It was no part of Gurdjieff's teaching that objective understanding is easier to attain than the formulation of the type of generalization with which a natural science is concerned. On the contrary, he taught that it was necessary to work far harder, and to work not only with one's mind, but with the whole of one's being, if such understanding were to be attained. Moreover, this work must be whole-hearted, undaunted by the seeming impossibility of the task. If man has two destinies—to serve the *Trogoautoegocrat* and disappear as an individual in the process, or to become an immortal soul of cosmic significance—there is no suggestion that the two paths are equally easy to follow. "To cross into the other stream is not so easy—merely to wish and you cross." On the contrary, the second destiny is reserved for those only who will endure to the end and never abandon the struggle. All this is expressed in the third principle described in the story of the Russian merchant, with his declaration that "if you go on a spree, then go the whole hog including the postage." If the second principle is a stumbling block to the intelligentsia, the third runs counter to the laziness and indecision inherent in everyone, and especially strong at the present time when our chief wish is that things should be made easy for us.

Stated in the abstract, I suppose that no one will challenge the assertion that everything really worth having must be paid for, or deny that if I really want something, I must be prepared to go the whole hog in order to get it. The trouble is that we do not really know what we want and have even less confidence in the possibility of getting it. We do not really believe that it is possible to go the whole hog. This can be seen very simply in the attitude of the Christian world to the Sermon on the Mount. The Sermon on the Mount can be very well described as a recommendation to go the whole hog in pursuit of the Kingdom of Heaven. It is commonly said that "if only" we could live even approximately according to the Sermon on the Mount, nearly all our human problems would be solved, and this world would become an earthly paradise. But the "if only" is looked upon as an insuperable obstacle. The Sermon on the Mount makes "impossible" demands upon human nature. Only a few rare individuals make the supreme effort to put its injunctions wholly and without compromise into practice. It is true that for human nature such as we know it, it is impossible, but we know that human nature can be changed. That is what "Christians" do not understand and do not want to understand, for it would place them under an obligation to go the whole hog in order to achieve it.

What is now lacking in the world is faith and hope. People do not believe in that reality which is designated by the term Kingdom of God, and even if they have a half faith, they do not have a real objective hope of attaining it.

Instead of the real objective hope that he can change his own nature by his own efforts, a man is taught to entertain all kinds of illusory hopes which remove from him the impulse to go the whole hog in pursuit of a new being. One of Gurdjieff's most remarkable powers was his ability to implant in those who came into effective contact with him the strong and lasting faith that the higher destiny of man is something real and to give each one personally the hope that he could attain it by his own endeavours. Such an inner certainty could only come through the growth of one's own understanding: and the seed of understanding is sown by "The Arousing of Thought."

THE SCENARIO

Beelzebub's Tales is constructed in the form of an allegorical tale of Beelzebub, represented as an angel who in his early youth revolted against what appeared to be to him some mistake or injustice in the ordering of the Universe. Instead of trying to find out the true reason he thought he could put it right himself. As a result of this much cosmic damage had been done, and because of this it was necessary for him to be exiled to the remote solar system Ors, of which the Earth is one of the planets. In this narrative, Beelzebub is supposed to have settled on the planet Mars and to have been provided with the means of travelling from one planet to another. Various of those who had been exiled with him had settled on different planets and some had settled on the Earth. All this happened before the time of the disappearance of Atlantis, in the early period of our human race, when there were beings of the tribe of Beelzebub living on the earth. The first time that he came to the earth was in response to an appeal from one of these beings who had rather rashly attempted to intervene in the affairs of the Government of Atlantis, feeling that injustice was being done on Atlantis, because he felt that the levying of taxes was causing great hardship. He was sure that by appealing to the "better nature" of the Atlanteans the needs of the State could be provided without imposing taxes. He persuaded the king to let him take over, giving his own personal guarantee that the revenues of the state would not suffer by this. They did suffer so much that he had to borrow money from all his relatives, and finally Beelzebub, who was the leader of the tribe, was asked to come to the earth and put things right. The only way to do so was by getting all the people of his tribe to assume responsibility for the task of putting things back where they were before.

The lesson here is that mankind has not reached the stage where appeals to our "better nature" will prevail over our egoism. Much time passed, and Atlantis disappeared into the waters and there was a fresh configuration of continents on the earth. After the disappearance of Atlantis, some who had saved themselves or had happened to be travelling in other continents, had formed settlements which had grown important especially those around the Persian Gulf. Various civilisations had been established. But there arose in these civilisations the custom of animal sacrifice, and this custom was regarded by the Higher Powers as producing certain radiations dangerous and harmful for the whole solar system. It therefore came about that the same archangel Looizos who had engineered the organ *Kundabuffer* appeared in Mars and raised the whole question with Beelzebub saying "you know something about the earth and its inhabitants. Do you think that without having to make a fresh disturbance of the whole cosmic equilibrium you could find some way of diminishing this custom of animal sacrifice on the earth, which is a most terrible thing?" In order to try to help in this Beelzebub came to the planet Earth several times and undertook this task by different means which are described in a series of anecdotes which typify the different ways in which people can be influenced. The method of external organisation to alleviate the lot of people having proved unworkable in the next three descents, Beelzebub shows how purely by the force of ideas a difficult situation can be changed. Here Gurdjieff anticipates the modern discovery that ideas can be spread among people so as to change the lives of people quickly and on a large scale.

Interspersed in these various chapters are many teachings about the general cosmological theory on which Gurdjieff's system is based. He starts from the idea of the world Universe which primitively was one single Supersun and by the very nature of existence necessarily passes through a process of gradual irreversible dispersion, of the kind that we associate with the flow of time.

Gurdjieff uses, without ever explaining it, the term *Merciless Heropass* to designate the flow of time. It reminds one of Zurvan in the middle Zoroastrian doctrine from which Gurdjieff probably derived it.

In order to correct this tendency towards the gradual dissolution of the Supersun, which he calls the Most Holy Sun Absolute, a fresh creation was made whereby the Universe as we know it appeared with its galaxies and stars. In this Universe the process of dispersion was replaced by mutual feeding, which Gurdjieff calls the *Trogoautoegocratic* process. This brought with it fresh consequences, that is, the Universe once having been launched in this way into the process of development, was expanding and developing and therefore becoming more complicated and thus its unity was threatened. Whereas its very coherence was threatened by the first process of the flow of time — that action that modern physics calls the Second Law of Thermodynamics — the second process threatened to make it impossible that the Universe should exist as an organised coherent whole. Therefore something new had to enter the Universe which could balance this process. This was the appearance of beings who could become independent individuals, whose own conscious action should bring the principle of unity, of coherence, into the Universe. This new factor was not introduced by the Creator of the Universe, because had the Creator intervened to bring this about He would have nullified the value of the second process.

BEELZEBUB AS HISTORY

ll the achievements of the historical period, including the advances of science and technology in recent centuries, are but child's play compared with the transformation in the human situation which occurred at the end of the Glaciation of Wurm. Not only did a new species of man appear with the forerunners of all our modern races already fully differentiated, but the new species, Homo Sapiens, looked with new eyes and wrought with new hands upon the world. He became concerned with the problems of human destiny and with the enigma of death.

No concept of history can be valid which cannot give account of its prodigious opening chord. Whether regarded as myth or as legend, *Beelzebub's Tales to His Grandson* lack nothing of the dramatic element in what he calls the First Transapalnian Perturbation and the deliverance of mankind from the shackles of the organ *Kundabuffer*.

For thousands of years, history continued until its interruption by the Second Transapalnian Perturbation, which he describes as coinciding with the disappearance of Atlantis. The very name Atlantis has had a strange fascination since the story taken from some unknown source was preserved by Plato in the *Timaeus*. This fascination is often ascribed to a naïve desire of man to look back to a Golden Age, the reality of which in the past might be a presage of its possible return in the future. Until recently, it has been regarded by most scholars as a myth invented by Plato for didactic purposes, and no less fanciful than that of Erech.[4] There is, however, an accumulation of

---

[4]*Republic*

geological evidence that between ten and fifteen thousand
years ago, changes in the level of the ocean occurred which
would correspond to the submerging of equatorial land masses
in the Atlantic Ocean.[5]

In Gurdjieff's own writings,[6] he refers to a legend transmitted from remote antiquity, which is even older than the
legend of Gilgamesh, and refers to the loss of Atlantis. If this
can be traced in the cuneiform writings in the Sumerian and
Babylonian records, it would be a striking confirmation of
Beelzebub's story of Atlantis. I am not, however, really concerned in the historicity of the Atlantean myth. Its importance
lies in the dramatic concept of a catastrophe, the relics of which
were those cultures which arose in Africa and Asia eight to ten
thousand years ago. Gurdjieff brings to the legend the vivid
picture of what he calls the Akhaldan Society, to convey the
idea of what can be discovered by men who make it their task
to search for objective truth and transmit to posterity the
results of their quest.

The third dramatic moment comes six to eight thousand
years ago with the period of great winds, resulting in devasta-
tion of great areas of the Gobi and Sahara, bringing about the
destruction of civilisations and great migrations of the peoples
of the earth. It was also the time when the region which is now
Abyssinia was a great centre of the world's culture, afterwards
transferred to the Valley of the Nile and thence in turn to
Mesopotamia.

At this point, Gurdjieff's story of mankind takes on a new
character. Whether or not he intended a literal historical interpretation to be given to his account of the earlier periods, there
is no doubt that he looked upon the early Mesopotamian civilisations as having unique significance for the subsequent life of

---

[5]See also George Poisson, *L'Atalantide Devant la Science*, 1945. Poisson, a
former president of the Société Préhistorique Francaise, has collected impres-
sive evidence in support of the theory that the Atlantean myth has an historical origin.
[6]G.I. Gurdjieff, *Meetings with Remarkable Men*, Chapter I (New York: Dutton,
1969; and London: Routledge & Kegan Paul, 1963).

mankind. In conversation, Gurdjieff often referred to what he called the Tikliamishian (that is, the Sumerian) civilisation as representing the highest level of culture which mankind had reached. He was referring, of course, to the balance between the inner and the outer life of man. In the final chapter of *All and Everything*, where he compares human life to a river which, when a man reaches a responsible age, divides into two streams, he speaks of this condition as of comparatively recent origin and says that in the Tikliamishian civilisation[7] there was no such division. In the context of the chapter, this means that the preparation for responsible age was accomplished in such a way that the young man or woman on reaching adulthood already understood the sense and meaning of his existence and could set before himself the aim of his life.

I remember myself the strong impression made on me many years ago by reading an account of a burial chamber in Akkad where some forty people had lain down peacefully in the prime of their life to die together, evidently undisturbed by anxiety as to the consequences of death. Although at that time I was unaware of the special significance which Gurdjieff attached to the Sumerian culture, I then felt that such assurance in the face of death could only come among people who understood the meaning of work upon themselves and knew how to prepare for it.

Gurdjieff's insistence that the principles and methods of work for self-creation were known in ancient Babylon had an obvious practical motive. He never claimed that the methods which he taught were invented by himself, but clearly indicated in the Second Series of his writings that he had derived them from diverse sources ranging from Abyssinia to the Far East. As I have already said, this diversity of origin has resulted in differences in the form of presentation which at first seem to imply differences of inner content. On closer examination, however, a single structure is disclosed. This means either a

---

[7]G.I. Gurdjieff, *All and Everything, Beelzebub's Tales to his Grandson* (New York: Dutton, 1973; and London: Routledge & Kegan Paul, 1950). Hereafter referred to as *All and Everything*.

work of synthesis on the part of Gurdjieff himself, or a common origin behind the diverse sources on which he drew. Comparing his teaching of the period from 1915 to 1918 as described by Ouspensky, and his own presentation fifteen years later in *Beelzebub's Tales*, there are clear evidences of a work of clarification, but the underlying unity was present from the start. It was this connectedness, indeed, which first made a powerful impression upon Ouspensky[8] and drew him to the study of Gurdjieff's ideas. It was the same with those of us that first met them in the early 1920s.

In so far as *Beelzebub's Tales* are a history of the inner experience of mankind, they show one main stream beginning, as I have said, with the Akhaldan Society which was dispersed after the loss of Atlantis and divided into three branches one of which developed first in Africa and later in the Middle East, while the second started in Central Asia and subsequently moved to China. The third reached India. The Eastern and the Egyptian traditions re-combined, or, at least, met again in Babylon, which thus became the repository of all the ancient wisdom. With the downfall of the early Babylonian Empire, the tradition was taken by schools to Central Asia and has there been preserved down to our day.

Gurdjieff thus presents history as having reached one of its nodal points in the Babylonian epoch. This perhaps explains why in *Beelzebub's Tales*, later history is treated less seriously, and we have only disparaging references to Greece and Rome and the satirical account of modern Western civilisation. Babylon is represented not only as the collecting point for ancient tradition, but also as the source of the division of human culture into the categories that we now call philosophy, art and religion.

The original purpose of the artistic activity was itself the transmission of ancient wisdom in such a form that it could be transmitted to a remote posterity.[9] Philosophy, which began as

---

[8]Ouspensky, *In Search of the Miraculous*, p. 28.
[9]*All and Everything*, p. 459.

the search for the laws of world creation and world mainte-
nance, degenerated into "wiseacreing" of minds clouded by the
illusion that knowledge could be acquired without "conscious
labour and intentional sufferings." Religion — which in the
hands of the "Wise King Konuzion" had been a weapon for
arousing in people unable to see for themselves the true prom-
ise of their destiny, the realisation of the necessity for a strenu-
ous purposeful life — [10] usurped the place of true knowledge and
severed mankind from contact with its natural leaders. These
are the true initiates who had perfected themselves by conscious labour and intentional suffering to the degree of the
Objective Reason which made them fitted to guide the destinies of man.

We have, finally, the second main theme of *Beelzebub's
Tales*. The first, as I have said, is the awakening of man to a
realisation of the significance and purpose of his existence. The
second is war, and the disastrous consequences which flow
from it for the life of mankind. A famous writer who read
Beelzebub's Tales in manuscript many years ago, described it as
the finest pamphlet against war which had ever been written.
And indeed, no reader can fail to be impressed with the sincere
feelings of horror and pity with which Gurdjieff regards this
most terrible scourge of human life. In his own autobiographi-
cal writings, Gurdjieff describes how in the early years of the
present century, his personal experience of war in every coun-
try aroused in him as a "second idée fixe of his inner world" the
need to understand the causes of war. War and Revolution!
Throughout history, this "periodic process of reciprocal
destruction" has intervened to make impossible that state of
progress towards an increased understanding which should
come through the efforts of wise and disinterested persons,
whose discoveries are preserved and transmitted for the benefit
of subsequent generations.

War is both unnecessary and unnatural, although a cosmic purpose is served by the life and death of beings on the

---

[10]*All and Everything*, p. 213.

earth. In one passage, Beelzebub explains to his grandson that if such a necessity as the premature destruction of life had once existed, this had long ceased to be the case and, on the contrary, it was now not only a disaster for man, but a disturbing factor in the economy of Nature.[11] The energy required for the equilibrium between the earth and the moon is not measured by quantity alone, but rather by quality. The needs of the cosmic equilibrium can far better be provided through the conscious labour and intentional suffering of three-brained beings striving for their own perfection than by premature violent death.

Of the causes of war, Gurdjieff gives his own characteristic account. Both in the Moscow conversations with Ouspensky and also in *Beelzebub's Tales*, he disregards the so-called political causes, the fears and ambitions of states and their rulers, the pressure of population and the working of economic laws. The mass hysteria which takes possession of peoples at times of war and revolution is the cause and not the consequence of the political event. The mass hysteria itself is the reaction of mankind to an influence which does not arise in human life. It is picturesquely described in a conversation in *"In Search of the Miraculous,"* where Gurdjieff speaks of stopping war and says, "What is war? It is the result of planetary influences. Somewhere up there, two or three planets have approached too near to each other; tension results. . . . With them it lasts, perhaps a second or two. But here, on the earth, people begin to slaughter one another and they go on slaughtering, maybe for several years. It seems to them at the time that they hate one another; or perhaps that they have to slaughter each other for some exalted purpose; or that they must defend somebody or something and then it is a very noble thing to do; or something else of the same kind. They fail to realise to what an extent they are mere pawns in the game." In *Beelzebub's Tales* this state of tension is given the name Solioonensius. In the Third Series of his writings, Gurdjieff says that he first learned this word in Africa

---

[11]*All and Everything*, p. 1115.

and that knowledge of the process and its effect upon the human psyche has been preserved from ancient Egypt. He illustrates it in the passage on Bolshevism which he compares with similar situations which occurred many times in the history of the Egyptian Dynasties.

Solioonensius can be compared with the atmospheric condition resulting from sunspots. There is indeed evidence that the occurrence of sunspots does have an effect upon the human psyche. More recently, a psychological effect of the varying intensity of cosmic radiation has been observed and reported. I mention these not to suggest that astrophysics has or shortly may discover or rather verify Gurdjieff's law of Solioonensius; but rather to emphasize that it implies nothing supernatural or mysterious. A similar, but more local effect and one which operates on a small scale and for short time is that of the direction of the wind. In England, the east wind, in Mediterranean countries, the Sirocco, have a peculiar and unmistakable effect upon people's nerves. When the east wind blows, most people become irritable and nothing seems to go right. I once became interested in this because I wanted to see whether it was a real or an imaginery effect. I asked a number of people to observe carefully and let me know as objectively as possible whether they could detect a state of inner tension caused by the east wind. Nearly everyone confirmed that a condition of irritability did in fact arise in them, even before they were aware that the east wind was blowing. I quote this for the purpose of illustration only.

Solioonensius acts not so much upon the sensing as upon the feeling brain in man. In a subtle and pervasive manner, great regions of the earth's surface, and sometimes the whole earth, become subject to a state of tension which produces in people the feeling of dissatisfaction with their conditions of life. They become irritable or aggressive, apprehensive, nervous and highly suggestible.

This does not, however, mean that Solioonensius is itself a harmful or destructive influence. According to Gurdjieff, it occurs upon all planets and is by no means characteristic of our earth alone. Dissatisfaction is no bad thing. Every imperfect being should be dissatisfied with his imperfection. On every planet where normal conditions prevail, the advent of Solioonensius is awaited with the solemn expectation that it will arouse greater determination and greater efforts of conscious labour and intentional suffering.

This is the great lesson that must be learned on the Earth. External dissatisfaction only leads to external conflict but no other dissatisfaction is possible in people who have not understood the sense and meaning of their existence. It can, therefore, truly be said that there is only one way to remove from among mankind the scourge of war, and that is to make people understand that their own existence as men, and not as things doomed to perish, depends upon the struggle for self-perfecting. Those who understand the necessity for working on themselves will then find in Solioonensius the very force to enable them to work harder. Those who have not themselves understood project their dissatisfaction outwards, become hostile and angry with other people, suspicious, jealous and open to every evil suggestion. They then become defenceless against mass psychosis. Fear and hate enter and distort the whole of their thinking and feeling. The very people who only a few years earlier could not conceive themselves consenting to the idea of war become involved in the destruction of human life.

It is not only human life that is destroyed by war, but the accumulated wisdom and experience which could make life more tolerable.

I have laid emphasis on war, because Gurdjieff in many passages calls it the greatest shame of human existence, a horror unprecedented in the universe.[12] His view of history would not, however, be completely stated without reference to his attitude towards distinctions of nation and class. He makes it clear that the normal planetary existence should be that of a single world government and the relations between people should be determined only by their qualities of being and not by accidents of birth.

---

[12]See in particular the chapter "War" in *All and Everything*, pp. 1055–1118.

The Reconciling Force In History

here are various ways of explaining why modern man is unable to perceive reality. All can be expressed as "consequences of the properties of the organ Kundabuffer." They result in a species of blinding which consists in seeing at most two of the three aspects of every situation. This Gurdjieff calls third-force blindness. It is the source of the dualistic propensity of all our thinking.

When we look around us, we usually see the world from one point of view—our own—and we deny either value or validity to any other. When we make an effort to be "impartial," we look for two opposing views and try to give equal weight to each. We seldom succeed because, obsessed with the dualism of "good" and "evil," we cannot help attaching these labels to one side or the other, according to our subjective likes and dislikes, our feelings of approval and disapproval.

Our dualistic propensity pursues us even when we are not confronted with such a choice. We see before us a situation we dislike and instead of striving to discern the factors from which it has arisen, we compare it with a non-existent situation which we conceive as desirable or even ideal. We compare what is, with what ought to be. We may picture to ourselves a perfect society, a world government, a universal religion, and criticize existing institutions in terms of our ideal picture. We may see the harmful and destructive processes which arise from divisions of race and class, and wish to see a world in which all men are equal. Utopias have always fascinated mankind just because of this inherent dualism. We see an abuse and desire to see a state of society from which it is abolished.

We have to divest ourselves of the whole attitude inherent in these tendencies before we can begin to see and sense reality. Many readers, whose susceptibilities have survived the reading of a thousand pages of *Beelzebub's Tales*, are nevertheless taken aback when they reach the statement that the idea of good and evil is the greatest human misfortune — "On the one hand a tranquilliser and justifier of all their manifestations and on the other hand the fundamental impeding factor for the possibility which arises in certain of them for the self-perfecting of their higher being-parts."[13]

Serious reflection must convince anyone that nothing obscures the sense of reality more effectually than to attach the labels "good" and "evil" to situations or tendencies. It is the falsification which destroys all religions, by removing the emphasis from the struggle for inward self-perfecting to an obsession with outward manifestations. I suppose that of all the teachings of Jesus Christ, few are more consistently ignored by Christians than the injunction "Judge not that ye be not judged."

One result of making judgments in terms of good and evil is the demand that things should be "changed." Some individual dislikes what is "bad" in a given situation and conceives in antithesis to it some ideal "good." This may lead him to start a movement to promote the "good" aim. His end point is a state of affairs ideally conceived, without reference to what is involved in the transformation. Almost without exception, the leaders of such movements refuse to take into account the existence of forces which must necessarily change the aim in the very process of its realisation, so that the outcome of their endeavours is always something unexpected and undesired.[14]

There are periods in history when the desire for change is not so strong or is at any rate confined to movements more or less free from violence. At other times, everything is unstable

---

[13]*All and Everything*, p. 1126.
[14]I have somewhat developed this thought in *The Crisis in Human Affairs*, Chapter II, "The Fallacies of Megalanthropism."

and the desire for conservation is relatively feeble. Then the movements of reform can easily become violent and destructive of all that is past.

Everyone agrees that our world today is not in a state of permanent stability. Some people hope and think that stability will be reached when mankind is fully permeated with the results of technical progress, and has adapted itself to the changed conditions of life which this will bring. To such a view, present instability is not a deeply serious matter, except for the danger that the policies of the great nations may fail to prevent wars on an increasingly destructive scale, which might annihilate the benefits of technical progress. The principal characteristic of such views is the belief in the adequacy of existing human institutions, that is, state governments working in conjunction with various international agencies to maintain order in the world — providing always that some "aggressive" group does not act to destroy the equilibrium.

People holding such beliefs may be compared to travellers on a raft who have committed themselves to the stream of a great river, confident that it will lead them to their destination, providing they are fortunate enough to escape destruction on passing through the rapids which lie between them and the broad valley ahead. The stream of the great river is the course of human history as it will proceed under the influence of existing general factors and the behaviour pattern with which mankind — being such as it is — will react to the situations that present themselves in the future. Struggle is necessary — even very hard work and much alertness — to keep the raft away from the rocks and whirlpools, but not for its propulsion or the determination of the general direction of its course. This position is that of naïve optimism, naïve in the sense that it assumes the combined general effect of all the factors at work is necessarily favourable to the hopes of mankind.

There is another and completely opposing view which holds that the very direction in which the world is going is that of inevitable disaster. The rocks and shoals before us are but a foretaste of conditions so disastrous, that our world must inevitably be destroyed unless we turn back before it is too late. The holders of such views are not necessarily or even often pessimists—for they usually believe that something can be done to change the course of the stream of events. It is true that they are generally unable to indicate with any clarity the positive direction in which they would wish events to move. An example can be seen in the advocates of world government. These hold that national governments must necessarily be exclusive, jealous and assertive and therefore unfitted to be entrusted with sovereignty, but they seldom have any conception of the way in which nationalism can be superseded.

The advocates of schemes for human betterment are for the most part dismissed by their contemporaries as unpractical dreamers and their activities have little or no effect. It is, however, common knowledge that "movements of reform" initiated in this way very often enter the stream of life through a change in the general attitude of mankind towards the particular question. The abolition of slavery, Universal Suffrage, State Socialism, the death of "imperialism" are all examples of tendencies which began as revolutionary movements or revolts against the existing order but, with a change in the general attitude of people, they have merged into the normal historical process. The struggle to produce a new stream of life moving in a different direction has always ended in furnishing only a new tributary which has swelled the waters of the ancient stream.

We have therefore to enquire seriously into the question of how anything different—not mechanical—can arise in the world. The Law of Threefoldness teaches us that for the realisation of an event there must be three independent factors. So long as a situation is conceived in dualistic terms, the third force cannot but operate accidentally, that is, without intention, and the outcome will not correspond to the desires and expectations of the participants. This is perhaps the best attested fact of history and until it is understood there can be no hope that the life of man can be made to correspond to its real objective purpose.

If we wish to pass from the dualistic to a triadic conception, we must find the independent third force. The principle is illustrated in *Beelzebub's Tales* by the account given of the origin of the Christian Lenten fast.[15] Beelzebub quotes from "an ancient Judaic-Essenian manuscript" which purports to give an account of a secret Council held at Kelnuk on the shores of the Dead Sea. The dualistic viewpoint is stated by the Greek philosopher Veggendiadi who affirms that to kill animals for the purpose of consuming their flesh for food is the greatest sin. Veggendiadi wishes to persuade all Christians to undertake a missionary campaign to abolish the practice of killing animals for food. The great Hertoonano, who is represented as a sage possessing wisdom of a higher order, accepts fully the proposition that the ideal state of affairs for man is that in which no flesh is eaten. "To cut short other lives merely to stuff one's own belly is an infamy of infamies such as only man is capable of. "Nevertheless, sober reflection must make it clear that the abolition of this infamy would only be possible if all the peoples of the world followed the same religion and were prepared to accept such a teaching. This being impossible, the only outcome of a missionary campaign would be the conversion of a limited number of people to the practice of abstinence from flesh food. But Hertoonano's researchers had established the consequences of such a situation would be that the abstainers who were living in contact with the eaters of flesh would suffer deterioration of their "will power" and that they would be unable to fulfil properly their obligations in life. The dilemma appears to be complete. To eat meat results in deterioration in the character; to abstain from it in the presence of meat eaters results in loss of will. Hertoonano shows that there is a way out. This turns upon knowledge of the specific effect of meat eating upon the character. It is due to the substance *Eknokh* the effect of which is harmful in certain months of the year. The desired results can therefore be fully achieved if a completely different objective is sought, namely the acceptance among the Christian peoples of the rule of abstaining from flesh food for forty days at a certain period in the year.

---

[15]*All and Everything*, p. 1016–1022.

The principle which this story illustrates is of vital importance for any practical undertaking or reform. An independent third force is brought to bear in the form of a new and deeper knowledge. There is no attempt to approximate to the original objective which is replaced by another which achieves the practical aim, though not the ideal situation. The essential distinction is between the unattainable ideal and the practical objective. The error lies in supposing that the practical objective can consist in the incomplete attainment of the ideal. It is an error because the incompleteness carries with it consequences which are bound to destroy the very aim which is desired. The practical objective is not to go some of the way along the ideal road, but to go all the way in another direction which leads to a situation that is inherently stable and can itself provide a starting point for a fresh move forward.

Throughout *Beelzebub's Tales*, examples abound of the right and wrong combination of forces. In the First Descent[16] Beelzebub is called in to redress a situation created by an attempt to establish a happy society through a benevolent despotism. The point here is that it is impossible to neutralise negative and destructive influences by pouring in material from outside. The objective pursued by Beelzebub's young kinsman is beyond the power of three-brained beings, even aided by superior resources from another planet.

The three tales of Beelzebub's successful endeavours to diminish the harmful custom of animal sacrifice, illustrate various ways in which the force of an idea can accomplish what is beyond the reach of a material agency. The objective must be limited and the idea must be brought into alliance with an existing tendency which has already a momentum of its own.

The story of the Kurd Atarnakh[17] and the method successfully devised by him for the prevention of war emphasizes the failure which must ultimately attend any project which

---

[16]*All and Everything*, p. 109.
[17]*All and Everything*, p. 1094–1104 *passim*.

involves the sacrifice of some principle necessary for the general or local cosmic harmony.

To understand how the reconciling force can arise, it is necessary to see that it cannot act in the same direction as either of the two opposing tendencies. It cannot be either an attempt to make the existing situation more tolerable or a movement towards a better or even the presumed ideal state. The only hope is to discover and press resolutely towards a different objective which will not be merely a half-way house to the theoretical ideal. Much energy is now being wasted in well-intentioned endeavours to do these very things. Such endeavours can only serve to perpetuate the existing conflicts and dangers. It appears simple and logical, having understood that war is an evil, to strive to remove the causes of war. More generally, it looks obvious that it must be right to enlist the "good" tendencies in man in support of "good" causes. **The underlying fallacy in all such projects is that they imply a conflict of good and evil which does not in fact exist.** The real conflict is between human aspirations and human powers. However much man may wish to resist the stream of events, he is unable to do so and his very struggles only serve to plunge him more helplessly into the current. The reconciling force must therefore be sought in that which can bring man's powers into harmony with his aims.

With this formulation we return to Gurdjieff's teaching. Man is powerless in his outer world and will remain so as long as he has no force in his inner world. It is only in the inner world of man that a reconciling principle can be found which will bring into harmony his desire for a better state and his actions which make that better state impossible.

It is necessary to distinguish between two apparently similar but really very different processes. The first is the striving to live in accordance with the significance and meaning of our own existence. The second is the striving to live to accomplish a purpose which we believe to be rightly conceived. The difference lies in this: that in the first case, we acknowledge from the start that we do not know the significance and purpose of our existence and seek to discover it. We do not know what we are or who we are or what it is we should become. We only have the conviction that these questions can be answered and are resolute in our determination to find the answer. In the second case, we assume that the answer is already known, the external objective defined, so that all that is required is to mobilise the forces to overcome the obstacles which prevent its realisation. In the first case, I start with a confession of ignorance, in the second with an assumption of knowledge. The first arouses in me the desire to change myself, the second the desire to change the world.

I have said enough to show that the desire to change the world leads to an external conflict in which there are of necessity unknown factors at work which will give a result quite different from what is intended. So long as I restrict myself to the struggle to change my own being, I can hope to gain sufficient knowledge of myself to reduce the unknown factors within manageable proportions and ultimately to eliminate them entirely. To change myself is a practical objective; to change the world is not merely an unrealisable ideal, it is violation of universal laws.

At this point, it may be objected that if I am only to change myself the main purpose is not served. The world is left to its own devices with the same dangers as before. To meet this objection, it is necessary to understand the practical meaning of the saying, "Seek ye first the Kingdom of God and His righteousness and all these things shall be added unto you." The Kingdom of God is the inner world of man and it is only there that the balance of the outer world can be redressed.

To understand how this can be so, we must return to Gurdjieff's question, "What is the significance and meaning of the life of man?" In "From the Author," he represents the two-fold destiny of man as corresponding to two streams of life, entering one of which a man remains helpless and is doomed ultimately to destruction. Entering the other, he can acquire his own imperishable being and pass to a different level of existence. This division into two streams is not natural; it is a consequence of a false understanding of what is important in life.

In the story of Ashiata Shiemash, Gurdjieff shows how the outer life of man can change as a result of a new factor entering his inner world. Ashiata Shiemash makes no attempt to influence the course of contemporary history. He does not even approach nor teach anything to the multitude, "as was done before and after him by all the Messengers sent from Above with the same aim."[18] He does not invoke the Sacred Impulses of Faith, Love and Hope, because he says that their distortion in human experience will produce results contrary to the aim. He therefore sets himself to work with a very small number of people, a few members of the brotherhood Heechtvori and thirty-five "serious and well-prepared novices." Having brought these few to understanding of the doctrine of conscience and having shown them how to work to bring their conscience into their waking life, he uses them to disseminate the idea that, "Only he who has conscience has in the objective sense the honest right to be called and really to be a genuine son of our COMMON FATHER CREATOR OF ALL THAT EXISTS."[19] The task of convincing others of this truth was then made a condition of membership of the brotherhood Heechtvori within which were preserved the secret teachings of Ashiata Shiemash himself. Thanks to this condition, the desire for the experience of objective conscience spread to an ever-widening circle of people, so that in varying degrees all began to work upon themselves to attain this experience.

The result of this work was to bring about profound changes in human relationships, and in particular the division into separate communities, that is nations, and various castes or classes ceased to exist. The striving for power gave place to the desire to manifest towards one another in accordance with conscience. With this war disappeared, or, as Beelzebub calls it, "The periodic process of reciprocal destruction." As soon as

---

[18]*All and Everything*, p. 348.
[19]*All and Everything*, p. 368.

mankind began to produce by conscious labour and intentional suffering the sacred substance Askokin, the death of beings no longer remained necessary on the same scale as before. The length of life increased and the birth rate diminished, so that a more harmonious and natural existence became possible.

The description given of the results of the labours of Ashiata Shiemash is clearly intended to show how a reconciling force can arise in the life of man. Ashiata Shiemash did not set himself directly to combat the typical abuses of human life, the hatreds and oppressions which lead to war and revolution. He did not even set before his disciples any ideal of external behaviour or rules of conduct. He only taught them to insist on seeking in their inner world for the Sacred Impulse of conscience. The results of this teaching manifested in the change in the external conditions of life.

In the final chapter of *Beelzebub's Tales*, "From the Author," Gurdjieff sums up the whole purpose of the book in the following passage:

> The general life of mankind has been divided into two streams since the time of what is called the Tikliamishian civilization, which directly preceded the Babylonian civilization.
>
> It was just from then on that there gradually began to be and ultimately was finally established that organization of the life of mankind which, as every sane-thinking man ought to constate, can now flow more or less tolerably only if people are divided into masters and slaves.
>
> Although to be either masters or slaves in a collective existence among children, like ourselves, of the COMMON FATHER, is unworthy of man, yet thanks at the present time to the conditions existing which have already been thoroughly fixed in the process of the collective life of people, the source of which lies in remote antiquity, we must be reconciled to it and accept a compromise that, according to impartial reasoning, should correspond both to our own personal welfare, and also at the same time not

be contrary to the commandments specially issuing to us people from the "Prime-Source-of-Everything-Existing."

Such a compromise, I think, is possible if certain people consciously set themselves, as the chief aim of their existence, to acquire in their presences all the corresponding data to become masters among those around them similar to themselves.

Proceeding from this and acting according to the wise saying of ancient times affirming that "in order to be in reality a just and good altruist it is inevitably required first of all to be an out and out egoist," and also profiting by the good sense given us by Great Nature, each one of us must set for his chief aim to become in the process of our collective life a master.

But not a master in that sense and meaning which this word conveys to contemporary people, namely, one who has many slaves and much money, handed down, in most cases, by inheritance, but in the sense that a given man, thanks to his, in the objective sense, devout acts towards those around him — that is to say, acts manifested by him according to dictates of his pure Reason alone, without the participation of those impulses which in him as in all people are engendered from the mentioned consequences of the properties of the maleficent organ Kundabuffer — acquires in himself that something which of itself constrains all those about him to bow before him and with reverence carry out his orders.[20]

The reader may reach this point and say to himself, "This is all very admirable, but how can it create a new world?" Great processes are in motion, and they have acquired a momentum which no ordinary force can arrest. If a few people, or even many, are drawn towards Gurdjieff's teaching, how can their work, isolated from any great organisation, whether secular or religious, be expected to produce any results?

---

[20]*All and Everything*, p. 1235-6.

I think the answer to this is very simple. It is always the work of a few people that has changed the world. Ideas are powerful, not organisations. Nothing can be done by outward force—everything can be done by inner strength.

There are in the world the elements of this inner strength. They reside in the conscience buried in every man's heart. But they are mixed with negative and destructive forces—the consequences of the properties of the organ Kundabuffer—like a sauce which has turned. Everyone who is a cook and has had experience of making sauces knows how this happens. A sauce is an emulsion of watery and fatty components. Suppose that I am making such a sauce for sixty or seventy people with pounds of precious butter and dozens of eggs. It gets overheated and in a moment it has turned. This is a terrifying moment for an inexperienced cook. He loses his head and beats the sauce violently only to make things worse. A good cook pours a little cold water at one edge of the bowl and stirs quietly until in one little corner the sauce turns back again. The emulsion spreads through the whole mass until the sauce is right again. The first time a cook sees this done, it looks almost miraculous. It is the same with the world. Everywhere people are stirring violently to make oil and water mix. This cannot happen. The part of wisdom is to establish here and there centres in which right relationships can exist by the power of a common understanding of what is ultimately important. From such centres there can spread throughout the world—perhaps far more quickly than we might imagine possible—the seeds of a new world.

PART TWO

COSMOLOGY

HARNELMIATZNEL — BLENDING

ne of Gurdjieff's formulations of the law of three is: "the higher blends with the lower to actualize the middle; which becomes higher for the preceding lower and lower for the succeeding higher." This is known as *harnelmiatznel*.

When this formula is interpreted for the whole of existence, the word "higher" here means that which is beyond our knowledge, the world which we cannot reach with our senses, and the word "lower" means the opposite, the world we can reach wholly through our senses. We can for convenience call these the "spiritual" and the "material" world, but however far we may go we can be sure that we will never be able to grab hold of the spiritual world and subject it to our gaze. For us, it is always beyond. We can be touched by it, feel its action, even have glimpses of it and become more and more convinced that there is a reality of that kind but we cannot bring it into our knowledge the way we can the content of this visible world.

There is a gap between the two worlds which is filled by their blending: by life. Life is totally different from the material world and totally different from the spiritual world. Both of these ideas are difficult to accept.

We know that all living bodies depend on the material energies for their functioning and it is said these days that life is simply a special form of material organization. This is totally wrong. Every living thing has something that material bodies do not have; every form of life, however simple, is sensitive. Because of this sensitivity, it has a power of selection which enables it to accept that which will nourish it and to reject what is harmful.

We should recognize that life is to be regarded as a distinct creation. Gurdjieff in the chapter "Purgatory" says that our Endlessness paid special attention to the emergence of aggregates of *microcosmoses*, the *tetartocosmoses*, capable of independent movement on the surface of planets.[1]

On the other side life is totally different from the spiritual world because it is subject to the limitations of space and time. It is sometimes said that the most primitive form of life, the blue-green algae or "primaeval slime" which has existed unchanged for two thousand million years, is immortal because it has never been born and never dies. This is right, but it is because the blue-green algae is not individualized at all, even in the form of cells. Every individualized life[2] is born and dies and birth and death are properties of life. Material things do not go through a cycle of birth and death and neither does the spiritual world.

Creative action is something that belongs to the spiritual world. It is outside of time and place; if it were not so then it would only be a matter of combinations. In creative action there is a **timeless action**. Such an action can enter us people but it cannot be said to be individualized in the way we think of life as individualized. If there were not this creative action, the world would be entirely governed by cause and effect, therefore essentially knowable and predictable, and this would mean in effect that there would only be the material world.

There is creativity, but it is not life and is not an attribute of life. Life did not create itself and no part of life creates itself.

We can understand the law of harnelmiatznel by taking a simple action from everyday life.

The material world is passive compared with us people. We can act on it. In that sense we are higher and the material

---

[1]In the early, unpublished version, this is connected with the search for food. A tetartocosmos is a living being with one, two or three brains; roughly speaking, an animal.

[2]Individualization arises with division; see also J.G. Bennett's *The Dramatic Universe*, Vol. I. p. 208, and Vol. IV. p. 134 (Ripon, England: Coombe Springs, 1977.)

world is lower, or we are more active and the material world is more passive. As an illustration let us think of the material world as a knife and of myself, or my activity, as my hand. The knife alone can do nothing: it cannot cut although its function is to cut. Also, my hand cannot cut although it wants to cut.

There is a loaf of bread to be cut. This loaf of bread can only be cut if my hand and the knife come together; if the higher blends with the lower. Then something new comes into existence which is neither my hand nor the loaf of bread, nor just these two together. We can call this the "cutting action." This is the **middle**. It is higher than the loaf of bread and lower for "me," that is, my intention.

In taking up the knife to cut a loaf of bread I have acted according to the law of *triamazikamno*. To understand this it has to be grasped that something has come into being that is more than just hand plus knife. Before they came together there was no cutting: the knife was a piece of metal and wood and behaved no differently from any other piece of wood and metal; it was inert. My hand had all the potential of what a human hand can do, but still there was no cutting. Cutting came only when my hand and the knife were blended.

We have to see that what comes through the blendings is a really new property.

When Gurdjieff says that the law of three is a **primordial cosmic law**, he means that it does not come out of the way that the world works but that it is a law that enables the world to be what it is.

To see that the act of cutting is something really new is as difficult as understanding what is meant by the Holy Ghost in the Christian Creed. Gurdjieff said categorically about this that man is third force blind, that is, man is not able without developing new perceptions to see the independence of the third force, even though it enters into everything that we do and see.

We tend to explain it away and say that to be active means to do things. We do not see that it is the third force that enables things to be done. It is not the active force nor the denying force that does anything. It is difficult to open ourselves to this yet it is not something remote.

To describe the differences of higher and lower Gurdjieff often uses the term **degree of vivifyingness**. Vivifyingness means life-givingness. It is not difficult to see that life is active for the material world and there should be no difficulty in seeing that life is an action, like the action of cutting, which is proceeding from some will or source beyond life itself.

Another way of looking at this is to think in terms of different media. We live in a medium of life and we live in a medium of materiality. We also live in a medium of something that is beyond life. There is something deeper than knowing within us that tells us that there is something more than the existence we are aware of. This something answers the question: "For what are we alive?" We can picture ourselves entering into the cutting and asking a similar question. When we come to see the loaf of bread and what is being done we begin to understand the answer.

Life cannot explain itself. Life depends on death and destruction; it is self-destroying. As we become more and more aware of life we see more and more how suffering and frustration enter into it. The more we look at it, the less we can see why there should be life. We need to come to the point where there is a working in us not just of life for the sake of living but of life for what life is for.

THE SIGNIFICANCE OF EVOLUTION

n thermodynamics, which is the study of the laws governing energy transformations in the material world, there is a law that amounts to saying that waste is inevitable in the transformation of energy from a lower to a higher grade. This was discovered about 150 years ago by Carnot. The realization that this was so gave rise to the feeling that eventually waste would predominate more and more; that is, energy would more and more move into a state where no useful work could be done with it. This feeling was given expression in Lord Kelvin's famous address in which he used the phrase "the heat death of the universe." The emotional feeling about the inevitable dissolution of all things—expressed so powerfully, of course, 2,500 years before by the Buddha—was given a new intellectual content. It seemed to be the fundamental law of the universe and later Eddington saw in it the very essence of Time.

Gradually, it has come about that it has been recognized that there is something quite different at work in the universe than this running down process. Parts of the world are hotting up, not cooling down, and life is admitted to have something different about it.

All these things were understood much better through direct insight by people who lived long ago. Gurdjieff certainly drew on these insights. The Merciless Heropass is undoubtedly an idea taken from the Zoroastrian teaching where it appears as Zurvan. Zurvan is beyond the control of the good spirit Ahura Mazda. It was by the creation of something, the Bull and then Man, Gayomart, that something was set up to prevent the inevitable destruction of the world.

We can put it in this way: as long as the world was looking along its own path, where things were going, then it had to be running down. When it began turning round and looking back towards the source, then the process of evolution could be started. When we forget to look back towards the source, we come again into the stream of destruction. In evolution, there is a reversal of forces which means a turning back towards the source. Something new is brought into the situation; it does not bring itself about.

The secret of our work is that it is a creative work, making what was not there before. This is what we people were intended to do. If we allow ourselves to be carried along by the stream of involution then we are truly going against the reason for which we were brought into existence. But it is extremely easy to go by the way of involution and extremely difficult to go by the way of evolution.

HARNELMIATZNEL —
TRANSFORMATION OF SUBSTANCE

n *Beelzebub's Tales*, the transformation of energies is called the *Ansanbaluiazar*. It is in the nature of this existing world that there should be a constant interaction between the energies on different levels. The upwards and downwards movement of energies is called *evolution and involution*. In involution, the many come out of the one and in evolution, the many return into the one. To maintain these processes there are needed means whereby one kind of energy can act upon another. These Gurdjieff calls apparatuses or *being-apparatuses* and he says that we men are apparatuses, individually and as a whole. Without apparatuses, energies have no means of coming into contact with one another.

In the picture of the creation he gives in the chapter "Purgatory," Gurdjieff says that to permit the renewal of the Sun Absolute it is necessary to provide a means by which substances coming from outside could be available. Creative impulses, the *theomertmalogos*, are sent outwards to act on the sub-material, prime source cosmic substance *etherokrilno* which produces a response by its very own divine nature. From this there comes the concentrations and different worlds and these worlds are the sources for the return to the one source. The whole of this process of transformation is called ansanbaluiazar and the evolution and involution of substances within any cosmos is also called by the same word. Ansanbaluiazar makes possible the reciprocal feeding by which everything is maintained, the trogoautoegocrat. In the unpublished version this was indicated by the word *fagologiria*, the reversal of forces by eating and being eaten.

First working

Second working

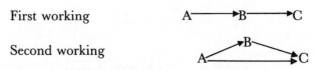

Figure 1. The Law of Threefoldness

The trogoautoegocrat was made possible, Gurdjieff says, by changes in the functioning of the law of threefoldness. In its original form, the law was simply a successiveness; one thing arises out of another and passes into a third. Then it was altered so that something new could arise. This can be roughly shown in figure 1.

There is now a difference in the role of the three forces. There is a place where two paths meet (C), one place where a path goes into a succeeding one (B) and one place where it all starts (A). This gives an end point, a transitional point and an initiating point.

It is this change of working that enables something to be concentrated at a point.[3]

The initial impulse coming from the *Sun Absolute*, the theomertmalogos, is destined to produce an independent creation and this must have its own spiritual life or freedom and is therefore the carrier of the third force. From the very start there is an invoking or forseeing of the end to be reached.

(1) theomertmalogos ————————►independent creation (3)

To arrive at this creation, the creative act has to pass through a receptive or denying force. This gives the form of action symbolised by the formula 1-2-3: affirming-denying-reconciling.

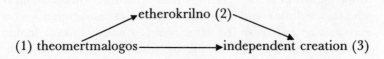

---

[3]Mr. Bennett also spoke of the reversal of one of these forces. This requires a different diagram from the one shown here.

We can say that from the start one is looking towards the end as an idea and one is moving towards the end as a fact. There is an ideal path and a factual path. When, in the great cosmic triad of world creation, the end is reached and the second order suns arise, there is not only the fact of their existence but also something of the vivifyingness of the original source in them. The sun is not just a concentration built up from the primary substance etherokrilno but also a reproduction or projection of the prime source. It is both a created thing and a creator.

The same applies to our arising. We have on the one hand our generation from the material world, from the physical and chemical substances out of which our bodies are produced and on which we feed; and on the other, we have the descent into the human essence of a spiritual nature. A simple way of putting this is that we are built up from below and spiritualized from above.

Apparatuses made in this way by a creative action of involution (1-2-3) are also apparatuses for the contrary movement of return to the source, evolution (2-1-3). The movement of return begins from below. This is why the work of our transformation begins from the material side of our nature. Primarily it begins in the physical body.

Where a finer substance arises out of the coarser one it is given the special name *harnelmiatznel*. The idea of harnel-miatznel, the higher blends with the lower to actualize the middle, is used extensively in the chapter on "Purgatory" to describe the process of transformation of food in the organism. It is said, for example, that when the food enters the mouth it mixes with the active elements produced in the body, the enzymes of the saliva, with which it combines according to the "affinity of vibrations" to give *protoëhary*. The affirming force must correspond to the denying force. The ferments and enzymes that enter into the digestive process are highly specific; they work on particular carbohydrate structures; one will hydrolyse a sugar, another a fat and so on. If the passive element is to be transformed it must meet with the precise active element that corresponds to its need, at that place and under these conditions. It is like the opening of a locked door; with no key it cannot open and with the wrong key it cannot open.

The need for a correspondence between the active and the passive principles applies to involution as well as to evolution. Let us take a very simple kind of involution, a fire. A fire is started and it requires fuel. The flame by which the fire is initiated can only go on as long as there is combustible material and air. The fire is helpless to reproduce itself unless the materials are available for it.

The further stages of the transformation of food also proceed by harnelmiatznel. The *being-protoëhary* passes into the intestinal tract. Here it blends with various ferments to actualize something active enough to pass through the membranes of the alimentary canal into the bloodstream. The new "middle" substance, the *being-defteroëhary*, yields the materials out of which the body's needs can be met. A part goes "to serve the planetary body itself", sugars to be burnt and substances to repair tissues; the rest passes through a further stage of evolution by the action of more specialized hormones to form the *tritoëhary* which is concentrated in the liver. The liver is a special organ in all chordate forms of life, not only vertebrates. In the liver food becomes alive and part of us; it is, so to say, resurrected. There is in the liver a combination of substances that produce the simplest living forms, as they were produced at the beginning of life on the earth. That is why in certain traditions the liver is regarded as the centre of man; these traditions knew about the transformation of energies.

It is at this point that the harnelmiatznel can no longer carry the process forward unaided. At this point we pass from the law of threefoldness to the law of sevenfoldness. The law of threefoldness cannot ensure the completion of the process and there has to be something brought in from outside. The places where this kind of thing has to happen are called *mdnel-in*, ways in. Such a place is reached when the food comes in the venous blood to the liver and help is given from outside by the air we breathe.

Air, our second food, belongs to a higher order of energies than the food we eat. The food we eat has to go through various stages of transformation before it is on the same level as air. The blood from the liver is carried into the network of capillaries in the lungs. Then there is neither a process of evolution nor of involution. A kind of reinforcement is received from the air whose potential for transformation is greater than that required for its own harnelmiatznel.

Always in the harnelmiatznel something is built up from below to meet something from above. The principle applies in procreation. The initiating factor is in the egg, the ovum. It cannot fertilize itself and needs the sperm. There is the apparatus of the sexual function that enables the two to be brought together.

In the mother is the aim that the egg should be fertilized. This is represented 2→3. From the aspect of the apparatus, there is the necessity for coming into contact with the active force represented by the sperm:

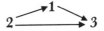

Harnelmiatznel also applies to the working of this school.[4] Those who come have a certain need; they come in order to get a certain development. The development is only possible if there is an apparatus and that is why schools exist. If this school possesses the right teaching, the harnelmiatznel will be set up. If it does not correspond to the need, or if those who come do not correspond in their potential, the harnelmiatznel will not be set up.

Similarly, there will not be a fertile mating unless the male and female principles correspond to each other. It is said that an action can come about only at the right time and place and with the right components.

The initiative in harnelmiatznel comes from the passive. In sexual reproduction it is that the woman attracts the man. In the case of a school like the Academy, if the initiative comes

[4]The International Academy for Continuous Education.

from the school and not from the students, harnelmiatznel is not set up. Instead there may be a process of involution. Such processes are necessary in other circumstances such as the spreading of a powerful idea in the world. Then the initiative is with the affirming force. If there is a sufficiently powerful potential in an idea it is only necessary to find situations to respond to it. The idea takes hold where there is "fuel" to burn; and gradually dies away as fires die away. That is why ideas in the world have to be renewed from time to time and no teaching can be permanent.

A School is different. It is concerned with providing conditions for evolution. The initiative must come from the seekers.[5] In so far as we are seekers, we can enter into harnelmiatznel. When our searching stops so does harnelmiatznel and there is no further progress. The seeker must have a strong feeling of need, corresponding to which there is a goal to be attained. Then it must be found out whether there is a correspondence between what the School has to teach and what the seeker is able to learn.

The harnelmiatznel will go only so far. But it requires different ferments at different stages, or different kinds of action. Otherwise the working of the School remains at the first stage (protoëhary).

If harnelmaitznel is a blending process the *harnel-aoot* is a disharmonized transition that Gurdjieff explained as resulting from alterations in two of the *stopinders* of the *heptaparaparshinokh*. It is the fifth point in the process of transformation and comes after the first mdnel-in.[6]

Here the vibrations are between the two extremes. Contact with the start has been lost and contact with the end has not yet been found. In the process of our transformation, this has been given names such as "Dark night of the Soul," but it

---

[5]In Sufism, they are called *salik* and the *murid* is one who is willing to lead.
[6]Every process that completes a transformation can be represented as an octave Do to Do where a tonality goes through various changes to the octave of its starting condition. In such a process, the middle point—the harnel-aoot—is Sol.

happens also on a small scale in little things, whenever we attempt anything. If the event is small, we may be carried through it by the momentum of some larger process.

When we try to attain something or learn something in depth there are at the beginning changes which come from putting things together by the process of harnelmiatznel; but when we come to the point of looking for perfection, for that which will really manifest the truth of what we are seeking, we are bound to come to a moment of despair when we feel we have no possibility of being able to find it or do what is needed. The harnel-aoot is a very painful experience but it is the only condition for reaching the perfection at which the process is aiming. In climbing a mountain, one must reach the point at which there is no feeling that it is possible to reach the top and no feeling that one can return to the bottom. Once that point is passed, no matter how hard the going is, one has the confidence of getting there in the end. The end itself becomes a force that is working in us. The process goes forward to the moment of completion, the second mdnel-in, when something else again is required.

One way of characterising the harnel-aoot is that here we have the separation between "I must" and "I cannot."

In describing the transformation of food Gurdjieff tells how after passing the *mechano-coinciding mdnel-in* there arises *tetartoëhary* and then *piandjoëhary*. Piandjoëhary is the fifth stage and he speaks in an extraordinary way about it, saying that it can give: "results not equal but opposite to each other." Piandojoëhary is a powerful substance in us and through it we are able to go further into creative work or we can be satisfied and put an end to the process there. In the further process, Piandjoëhary becomes *exioëhary* and finally *resulzarian* where the food has been transformed into a substance of the body *Kesdjan*.

The question then arises: what of the second mdnel-in? In none of Gurdjieff's talks or writings of which we have any record is it explained what is meant by the *intentionally-actualizing-mdnel-in*. Everyone has the feeling that here something more is needed than that the apparatus should work, something has to come from us that has something to do with sacrifice and suffering, Gurdjieff would never answer questions about this. In *Beelzebub's Tales* he simply says that it is here that the substances needed for the Higher Being Body or Soul, enter.[7]

---

[7]Gurdjieff in "Purgatory" simply says that here enters the "foreign help" foreordained by our Creator for our perfecting, that is, *being-partkdolg-duty* or "conscious labours" and "international sufferings."

THEOMERTMALOGOS,
ENERGIES AND ETHEROKRILNO

he language we have is based on our experience of this world. It is totally unsuited for talking about the invisible region. It has the disastrous effect of making us feel that we understand something. We borrow from the experience of this world to try and say something about what is beyond it.

We talk about God, but that word refers to something beyond our understanding. We feel a need to speak in some way of the Source from which we come and to which we must return; and of the Power that creates and guides the Universe. We begin to think of some being because we cannot imagine anything being done unless it is done by a being and then we are led to try and describe this being. In this way a totally fictitious science called theology has come into existence which is supposed to teach us about God, His attributes and qualities.

Because of the absurdities that result, some people fall into the trap of denying anything higher than themselves. They see the muddle and contradictions but get into a worse state of affairs.

When we use the word God we are using a word to stand for something which we cannot possibly have an idea of. Of all the great Teachers, the Buddha was nearest to expressing this. He constantly impressed on his followers that there was no way by which anyone can affirm or deny anything about the Supreme. Yet we are bound to say something.

It is possible to say a great deal about **energies** without being caught by misleading images. This had led people into making a different kind of mistake. People say that physical science has discovered that everything is energy and they say that thoughts and feelings and so on are also energies and so everything is energy and everything will be known in that way. It is not like that. There are different degrees of organization that cannot be expressed in terms of energy. There are the working of laws and the determinants of action.

One of the most important things we need to speak about is that there are different worlds. The simplest distinction we make is of a material and a spiritual world. This is really valid, but we can also talk about more than one spiritual world. Various teachings talk about seven heavens or seven regions. To live in the spiritual world one must be a spiritual being but there are different kinds of spiritual being. For men we can talk about different bodies of man, found in many teachings; natural body, spiritual body, divine body, resurrection body; astral body, mental body, causal body and so on. Sometimes it is said that man has two bodies, body and soul, sometimes three, body, soul and spirit, or in Gurdjieff's terminology the physical body, the *Kesdjan* body and the higher being body or the body of the soul. In the same teaching it may even be that the number of bodies talked about is different and there is a reason for that.

When Gurdjieff talks about his centres, sometimes he says there are three, corresponding to the instinctive and bodily functions, emotional and feeling function and intellectual function. Another time he distinguishes the instinctive centre in its own right, the body as it regulates itself, from the moving centre which has to do with the body acting in the external world. There are different nervous systems and anatomical locations which make this a valid distinction. Then Gurdjieff sometimes speaks of sex and a sex centre. The elaborate nervous system and the hormones and so on belonging to sex more than justifies this. So we start with three centres which then become four and then become five centres. At another point Gurdjieff will talk of two higher centres and even put them somewhere in a diagram as if they belong to totally different kinds of experience. So then we have man with seven centres. This is characteristic of Gurdjieff's method and by using language that is not fixed he increases the power of language considerably. We must not let ourselves be disconcerted by hearing about three centres one day, five another and seven another. The same thing applies to Gurdjieff's description of the bodies of man. Sometimes he even speaks of man as having only one body.[8] Whatever the description, it refers to something; but to try and reduce it all to a scheme where everything is pinned down is nonsensical. The different descriptions are just signposts to help us feel our way around, beyond the limitations of our understanding and consciousness. They are not really descriptions at all. They are more like evocations, arousing in us some sense of the different modes of experience that are possible. Perhaps they can help us organize our experiences as they come to us.

Each of the bodies of man enables him to live in a corresponding world. This is expressed in the parable of the wedding garment where it is said that a man cannot go into a world if he does not have the appropriate body or "garment."

We can also speak here of levels of consciousness. A common notion is that of the sleeping state and the waking state, but Gurdjieff in his psychology says that there is more than one kind of waking state. There is a real substantial difference between the dream state in which people spend most of their lives and the true waking state in which there is an awareness of direct contact with the natural world, when we are what we are and there is not a veil of dream between us and the natural order. It is possible to speak of states of consciousness beyond this higher consciousness; cosmic consciousness, objective consciousness and so on. Again, in different teachings different states of consciousness are described. It is said that these states fluctuate and that a man can be lifted up into another world by a change of consciousness. St. Paul describes his own experience of being taken up into the fourth heaven and being aware of things which cannot be known in ordinary states of consciousness.

Gurdjieff's use of the word "consciousness" is very changeable. Besides the notion of different levels of consciousness he

---

[8]Which may have some connection with the "sensation body" or "vehicle."

sometimes uses the word to mean our ordinary experience. A phrase like: "that consciousness in which they pass their ordinary lives" is saying pretty much the same as *personality* as distinct from *essence*. It is this consciousness with which you read these words.

Gurdjieff also spoke about objective and subjective consciousness, but in the later presentations used in *Beelzebub's Tales* he did not use this, but spoke about *gradations of Reason*.

Different degrees of consciousness can be connected with different energies and we can say that every energy carries with it a corresponding state or level of consciousness. We can also say that the different bodies of man are made with different energies and that they are capable of different states. But there is a danger here, too, in that we can begin to slip into ways of thinking in which everything is misunderstood. We can all too easily begin to think of a world as a place in which one is present, the state of consciousness as an awareness of whether one is in it or not and that a body is something that one has as a mark of one's own being. This happens when we put these ideas together in the same way as we put ideas concerning our ordinary experience together. Then we lose contact with their reality and our understanding is blocked.

We can be given something to enable us to stretch towards a different kind of understanding but still bring it back to something ordinary. People who have had the direct experience and feel the responsibility to convey something to those who have not yet come to it, are faced with an impossible task. They are in the situation of going from the whole to the part, but the people they want to speak to are still in the situation of separateness and they have to go from the part to the whole. People in the situation of separateness are bound to think in a spatial and temporal way such as we do in making maps of territories, plans of machines and anatomical charts of bodies. This not only blocks understanding but, more seriously, it thwarts the possibility of new kinds of experience. Even when an authentic experience comes it is thought about in terms of the old kind of picture. Things are put together in the old kind of way — as if they were separate.

The one thing that is not permissible when we are dealing with the spiritual world is to attempt to go from the part to the whole. The spiritual world begins from the whole, whereas the material world begins from the part.

It is said that it is useless to start from explanations and we must start from experiences; but the one thing that can be put in front of people is some idea of pitfalls to be encountered. In any study or search towards the reality of man, the universe or God or whatever aspect it is of the whole within which we are what we are, we will get lost if we lose contact with the whole. It is possible to practise making contact with the whole as a spiritual exercise.[9] The wholeness in which we share — for example, in getting together in a khalqa[10] — cannot be reduced to quantity. Two or three gathered together are just as much a whole as the whole of humanity.

The reason why the study of energies is so important can now be explained. It enables us to talk about the workings of the universe without having to talk about beings doing things, whether great or small, absolute, divine or human beings. Being is very very difficult to understand; the important point is that being means something only for a very short distance and one must get beyond it; but to understand non-being is too much.

Energies lie somewhere between and their study enables us to understand **action** in a right kind of way, without picturing it always as some being doing something. In our usual modes of thought we assume that being comes before doing or that being is somehow independent of action. In many actions, we look and see a number of people, say, who are trying to do something or who are doing something. The truth is just the opposite. **We** are nothing at all, it is the action which makes us. Our being is only an illusion; it is the action that is really there.

---

[9]Such as the making of the three *rukus*: obeisance to the individual, universal and absolute qualities of wholeness, though these words in spite of being very precise, do not convey what one might think they do.
[10]See also the section on Helkdonis, p. 1106.

We can hardly bring ourselves to see that there are doings who **be** things. If I say something it is not I that says it but that speaking says me. We can come to be aware of this if we observe ourselves well; then we can begin to understand that the world is an action of unlimited significance. Within this action there are beings but they are subordinate to the action.[11] It is the action that produces beings and when the action is completed, it dispenses with them.

Sometimes an artist gets a glimpse of this when he realizes that he is not painting the picture but the picture is making him an artist by creating itself through him.

The world is in the process of being created. This is the ultimate thing. It is not possible to say that the world is either creating itself or being created by something else. This we can come to understand through the study of energies.

First, there is the ground from which the world is created. Gurdjieff speaks about the "prime source cosmic substance." This is by no means a new or unusual idea. Modern physical science is finding it necessary to posit something which is not in being and yet out of which being can come. Whether people think of this in terms of a primordial state in the past, or something continuously happening throughout time, or something timelessly happening in a different dimension depends on the cosmological language they prefer to use. The prime stuff is always taken to be not yet sufficiently organized to be anything at all. It is neither radiation nor does it consist of particles.

The word that Gurdjieff used for this substance was *etherokrilno* in which the Greek word *etheros* is combined with the letters K and R which in many languages represents the creative power, as in the English word "creation." In the Arabic language KR or KRR is an important element signifying creative action. Etherokrilno means therefore the formless material in which the creative process can work.

---

[11]Gurdjieff puts this in terms of *being-apparatuses* for the transformation of energies.

At first this seems to be a fairly easy idea but it is not so. In reality it is a very difficult idea. As soon as we have given something a name we start believing that we are talking about something that is. This difficulty is obvious in the problem physical science has with talking about the ether and whether it exists or not. If it exists then it has properties and the point of it is lost and if it has no properties then it does not exist and therefore does not help us to understand anything. Etherokrilno is nothing in itself yet everything is made out of it.

Gurdjieff also speaks of a supreme organizing power, that which brings being out of the etherokrilno, the theomertmalogos, literally "the word from the mouth of God." This is beyond being. It is expressed in the Qu'ran: "Be and it was." Between the theomertmalogos and the etherokrilno there is an infinite action and for this action to take place something must connect them. This third element that is present is all the different actions of the world Gurdjieff calls the Holy Reconciling.[12]

In *Beelzebub's Tales*, Gurdjieff has the theomertmalogos coming from the *Sun Absolute*. The Sun Absolute is not a being, it is the completely unified source out of which the creative power emanates. He avoided using the word "proceeds" because this is generally applied to the third force.

The idea of the three forces is very ancient, particularly in the Indo-European tradition represented by the *Vedas*, which go back many thousands of years to a time when there was a very high wisdom in the world. Two or three thousand years ago the ancient tradition was re-expressed in the *Sankhya* school of teaching.[13] There one has the doctrine of the three *gunas*, but later on the original meaning was lost and the guna became connected with moral ideas and states of being. In the earliest notions of this, the gunas are simply the threefoldness through which all the differentiation of the world comes about. Difficulties have always arisen whenever this threefoldness has been

---

[12]This is spelled out in the early version of "Purgatory" but is not so clear in the published version.

[13]Founded by Kopila who must have lived before the sixth century B.C. though it did not flourish until much later.

put into terms of being. This was especially so in the Christian teaching. There was special difficulty in understanding the place of the second power, which was associated with the Incarnation. The schools of North Africa and Alexandria made a great contribution and there was inserted into the creed the declaration that the third force proceeds from the first and second forces. This third reconciling force makes it possible for there to be love in the creation. The reconciling action is required to complete the creative process, not at some remote time in the past, but perpetually and timelessly. This profound teaching was given side by side with ways of helping people with their lives, by providing them with motives for serving the cosmic purpose.

Gurdjieff's ideas are not in any naïve sense new, but they are presented in such a way that they are relatively free from other associations.

To return to the arising of the creation, we can picture the surface of the primeval ocean where nothing stirs until the creative power descends upon it. The first action is a striving in the etherokrilno that precedes its emergence into being. This striving was understood by the great sages, the *Rishis* of Vedic times as *Tapas*, the movement that produces differences. This means "warmth" or "heat," but the same word applies also to austerity and sacrifice.

This figurative language of an ocean upon which a creative power descends appears also in the beginning of the Book of Genesis where the strange word *Elohim* is used. The word has plural form and yet essentially expresses unity because of the syllable AL. The spiritual power that brings about the first movement has an equivalent in us. There is in the depth of our nature the potential for transformation by which we are able to enter into this cosmic action and in doing so, acquire our own being. Something has to start this off. There has to be the entry of the spiritual power into the soul of man. Here the word "soul" must be understood as something like the etherokrilno, as something that is not organized, simply a possibility of being something. When the spiritual power enters it produces in us the sense of privation.

One great Christian theologian, Meister Eckhart, did get beyond notions of persons or being. He saw so much and so deeply that it was impossible for him to convey what he had seen. From time to time this is revealed when something has to be brought into action. There are always people able to be aware of it sufficiently for continuity to be maintained. About a century or two earlier than Meister Eckhart, Gregory of Palamos, an Eastern monk living in Byzantium, also understood some extraordinary things which he was unable to express because they were too strange. Much earlier still there was that remarkable man Origen who was almost not regarded as a Christian at all.

One of the most significant notions that Origen expressed was of this privation, *sterisis*. This privation has been introduced into the cosmos so that **the creation can create itself**. If it were not aware of being separated from its Source there would be nothing to make it return to its Source. Hence, privation is the beginning of the creation.

It is possible also to look at the other extreme where the theomertmalogos penetrates into the world. Here privation is transformed into something quite different, the immediate need for union, for the final liberation from all that keeps us separate. Between the two are all kinds of intermediate states that constitute different kinds of working.

The word "energy" properly means a working, *energeia*. At school we learn that energy is the "capacity for doing work." What we need to do is to put together the notion that energy makes the action possible with the notion that energy is the action itself.

We know from physical science that we can talk of the amount or quantity of an energy and the intensity of energy and these are different things (such as the amount of heat and its temperature). We can also talk of the quality of energy and how energy of one quality can be transformed into another. The idea of quality was considered very deeply from another direction by Gregory of Palamos who used it very much in talking about the divine operations or energies.

When we come to the higher energies there is a wholeness that does not even have any parts. Even the notion of quality is not enough.

In the scale of energies from the etherokrilno as one limit to the theomertmalogos as the other there are different gradations which can be talked about in different ways: in terms of different worlds, different states of consciousness, different modes of being, different potentialities for playing a cosmic role and so on. This is not talking about different things, it is different ways of talking about the same thing. In the middle of the scale of energies there is life. We live in the midst of life. Life is really our natural world. We know that there are states below life, inertial material states. What we do not know is that there are states beyond life. They are very hard to conceive.

We know that life is organized in different ways. On the physiological level, blood and the human organism work like ordinary physical generators and motors and the muscles and so on are very much like the machines we ourselves make. When we come to the finer, spiritualized parts of man we begin to talk of a second body. For this *kesdjan* body, the "blood" is *hanbledzoin*. Hanbledzoin is one of the keys to understanding our inner and outer possibilities. Gurdjieff uses the word in many different ways. In the *Third Series*[14] he spoke about his decision to sacrifice his own power in the field of hanbledzoin, a power he was able to use for his own purposes. In another place, he speaks of hanbledzoin as the emanation of tetartocosmoses, understood as three-brained beings. Hanbledzoin is also said to be the substance of a higher body of man.

We know in the physical world that there are different energies and every machine needs a certain kind of energy or fuel to run. We know something about generators, which convert one kind of energy into another. Usually we think of

---

[14]G.I. Gurdjieff, *Life is Real Only Then, When "I Am,"* published for private circulation only.

them as having to be regulated and looked after by some kind of external consciousness, a human operator, and having to be designed and built by somebody. When it comes to the body we know that we do not construct it and for the most part do not know how to operate it. All that has to do with the transformation of energy for its functioning is done instinctively without any participation of our consciousness. When we look at our bodies we soon come to a point where it is very difficult to make a distinction between energy and the machine that uses it. The most important example of this is the blood where it is very hard to say what is the energy, what is the machine, what is the generator or what is the material on which work is done. Yet we imagine that we know what blood is. Even if we say that there must be substances in the blood that we have not yet detected and some action we have not accounted for, we still imagine that these will be like the things we do know.

One must be quite ready to give up asking what the word hanbledzoin and all such words "mean." We cannot deal with these things as we can with things of the physical world. Perhaps we have to go still further and give up asking about meaning altogether and realize that the very question implies a kind of division that must be short of the wholeness of things.

If we look at a tree and ask ourselves what it means it does not take long to see that this is a silly question. It is so with hanbledzoin. Hanbledzoin is really the action of the human essence.

Life is not only human and characteristic of this earth, it has the peculiar power of bridging the gulf between the separate atomic world of physical phenomena and the universal world beyond individuation, beyond being, the real spiritual world. Life is the bridge and we are part of life. Gurdjieff speaks of the threefoldness of the creation as a fundamental cosmic law. He calls this law *triamazikamno*, "I put three together." In the ultimate, cosmic scheme, the theomertmalogos is the holy affirming and the etherokrilno the holy denying.

The whole working of the universe, particularly through life, is the reconciling.[15]

Somewhere between the formless ground and the creative source there is a region occupied by some kind of self-sustaining, self-renewing existence that is capable of acquiring the kind of consciousness we people have. We can grasp that when we are conscious we have possibilities we do not have when we are unconscious. Maybe we come to see that there are different degrees, ranging from states no different from sleep to a consciousness in which we can really see what things are. But is there something beyond consciousness? It is difficult to ask this question seriously. It is the same as asking if there is anything beyond life — not just a higher, more organized kind of life, but something really different.

The reality we are searching for is beyond consciousness. We are not able to touch it so long as we are held by consciousness. Consciousness is a band in the middle with something below consciousness on one side and something beyond consciousness on the other.

---

[15]G.I. Gurdjieff, *All and Everything, Beelzebub's Tales to his Grandson* (New York: Dutton, 1973; and London: Routledge & Kegan Paul, 1950), p. 779. Hereafter referred to as *All and Everything*.

PART THREE

COSMOGONY

Holy Planet Purgatory, 1974
Merciless Heropass, 1974
Law of Sevenfoldness, 1974

HOLY PLANET PURGATORY

he world, man and God are presented in *Beelzebub's Tales* as a striving, as the shared undertaking of a task. The world is not a perfect machine producing predetermined results. The world has got something unbalanced or lopsided about it which makes correction necessary. This is where the drama of the creation begins.

In "Purgatory," a contrast is made between a world with perfectly adjusted laws and one in which always some adjustment, correction and intervention is needed. The first world is that of the *Sun Absolute*. At first glance, it is puzzling why the Sun Absolute should be decreasing in volume with time. What is meant by time or the *merciless heropass* we shall talk about later, but it is sufficient to say that for **anything to happen** time must be a factor.

There is a kind of static happening as we might envisage with a perfect machine that is self regulating, will not wear out and requires no energy sources from outside; where the end, a predetermined result, is there all the time. If events are so precisely adjusted that nothing is lost, nothing can really happen. If something is to happen, it means that other things are **not** to happen. If we speak, we cannot be silent at the same time. If we manifest in any way there is an enormous loss because of all the things that then cannot happen. This is what is meant by the diminution of volume. It is a diminution of possibilities.

We could, perhaps, look at the condition of the Sun Absolute as equivalent to a simple pendulum, moving without friction and drag, endlessly oscillating. But nothing would really be happening. There would be no way of having time as we

know it, for everything is then perfectly reversible. This is the
kind of image many people have of the divine world, but it is
not one that Gurdjieff would ever countenance.[1]

If we allow irreversibility, that is, definite change, then
eventually everything must come to a stop. At each successive
event, the possibilities that are open become more restricted.
The possibility of renewal had to be introduced.

Renewal does not make things simpler or tidier. It cannot
work in the way the laws of predetermination work. As Gurdjieff expresses it, it is clear that the modification of the fundamental laws introduces hazard into the whole business.

We can look at this in the action of evolution on our
planet. There was a period when life was governed entirely by
the simple laws of variation and elimination that Darwin
described. Then came the period when all this was upset by the
coming of man who was able to act against these laws. This
introduced quite new possibilities.[2]

If we were perfect animals living precisely regulated lives
there would not be a human world, nor an interesting or creative world. No doubt in many ways we are inferior or imperfect
animals. There is loss as well as gain.

This introduction of new possibilities gives a meaning to
success and therefore also to failure. This is something new. A
perfectly adjusted clock will tell the time perfectly until it runs

---

[1]This is the world of microscopic events. It has always been a puzzle in
modern physical science how the reversible processes of the microscopic
world conspire to produce a world of macroscopic events in which irreversibility is the rule (thermodynamic time). Many things said by Gurdjieff in the
"Purgatory" chapter point the way to understanding this. In the macroscopic
world there is an interaction between internal and external processes, which
are relatively independent. That is what it means to have a macroscopic
world. This, then, is just the same as the modification of the fundamental
laws—making them dependent on "forces from outside"—of which Gurdjieff
speaks.
[2]The introduction of new possibilities is a major theme in *Beelzebub's Tales*
which is in many respects a testimony to human, angelic and divine ingenu-
ity. But it must always be seen as something "open-ended," not a predetermined action seen in advance as part of the great machine.

down and is quite useless. There is no failure or success there. The price for something new to come into the world is uncertainty, danger and insecurity.

The picture given of the laws in the Sun Absolute shows them as independent and perfectly adjusted. The law of three, *triamazikamno* relates everything to everything else. The law of seven, *heptaparaparshinokh*, determines how we pass from one state to another. In its isolated and pure form, it is the law of cause and effect with no side-chains, no interactions: everything is perfectly predictable. In physical science, the law of three appears as the law of conservation according to which nothing is gained or lost in the material world. The law of seven appears as the law of irreversibility which says that in any exchange something is lost and that eventually all must come to a standstill or equilibrium. The two laws of physical science are known as the first and second laws of thermodynamics. They are expressed without any reference to intelligent interaction.

The great change coming about in twentieth century science is the recognition of uncertainty, the inexactitude and unknowableness of laws in the very nature of the existing world. We are being forced to see that there is something really wrong in supposing that if we know enough we can cope with any situation that arises. This has been found out in the use of digital computers which were introduced in the expectation that with such an instrument it would be possible to predict what was going to happen and eventually get control. It has worked out in quite an opposite way and we get into worse trouble using computerized prediction than in going by our hunches.

When Gurdjieff wrote Purgatory, people were still searching for new laws which would enable us to predict when the disintegration of an atom would occur and the like, that is, enable us to predict what seemed to be unpredictable. Now, we are more uncertain about these things and are beginning to acknowledge the uncertainty in the physical world and even more so in the world of life and far more so in the world of human life. The higher up the scale we go, the more we find uncertainty, unpredictability and hazard. What Gurdjieff wanted to bring out in this chapter was that this uncertainty goes all the way, even to the ultimate source.

Intelligence is something apart from the laws and introduces the "unforseeingnesses" of His Endlessness. With intelligence there can be feedback to the source and the way in which it works is through the arising of gaps or holes. This means that the law of seven will no longer work by itself, because there are hiatuses where something has to be introduced. In its pure and independent working, heptaparaparshinokh always completed its cycle in a predictable way.

Everything that happens in the physical world is possible only because there are holes. Take the simple thing of water flowing through a pipe or down a mountain in a stream. Flow would not be possible without the holes and discontinuities in the structure of water. With fewer holes there would be ice, but with no holes at all the ice would not even be breakable. In a world without holes, nothing could be done.

In the change of the working of the law, it is put that at some places gaps are opened, at other places things are brought closer together and at other places connections are uncertain and hazardous. The change in the working of the laws is the second stage of creation. It enables there to be some opposition and changes of direction and predictability had to be sacrificed.

One kind of uncertainty is that no one cause is sufficient to produce a result, there have to be side actions taking place. This is represented by the lengthening of the third *stopinder*. Another is that there have to be discontinuities in the completion of an action, represented by the shortening of the seventh stopinder, so that something can take over from the result, or "from the future." There is now a disharmony between the beginning and the end. This is felt at a certain place in the process of transition, the *harnel-aoot*, where the process is no longer connected with its source by a thread that holds it, nor is it connected with its goal by a thread that draws it.

The working of relationships is no longer something perfect where every part of the cosmos is perfectly related to the other parts; there is always the need for some kind of help. We do not encounter in this world any perfect triad, but always triads in which there is something missing that has to be supplemented from another triad. Instead of independent triads there are a network where each one depends on the others to hold it together.

So we have the change from *Autoegocrat* — "I keep everything under my control" — to *trogoautoegocrat* — "I hold myself together by feeding" (*trogo* — "I eat"; *auto* — "myself"; *ego* — "I"; *crat* from *cratizo* — "I hold").

Side by side there is now a perfect machine and an imperfect machine; one which is unconditioned and one which is conditioned. By their combination it is possible to set up a self-renewing process and "all fears of the eventual disappearance of the Sun Absolute were ended." This corresponds to a world that we can see, the world that we call the material universe.

It is said that originally the Wisdom of God, theomertmalogos or Word-God, only set the world in motion and thereafter it proceeded by mechanical laws. In the third stage of the creation it was necessary for the theomertmalogos to manifest as the third sacred force or the reconciling force. The theomertmalogos as third force enters where every second order sun is active and the other suns in relation to it are passive. In this action we have the distinction of outside and inside corresponding to World XII,[3] the world of individuality, that of the second order suns.

But if the intelligence of the Creator has to keep the world adjusted then it is not fulfilling all that is required. Intelligence has to enter into the world itself and the world has to become intelligent independently of God. This means that independent intelligences should take over more and more the work of adjusting the feedback or trogoautoegocrat so that the world can provide a living and immortal system within which the Creator can work.

---

[3]For this scheme of worlds, see also *The Dramatic Universe*, Vol. II, Chapter 29.

The second order suns are secondary creative powers, but they are conditioned. This is what is meant in the chapter by the words "lost half the force of their vivifyingness." The second order suns as we said, correspond to World XII and also to the individuality in each one of us. The third order suns or planets correspond to World XXIV and to the selfhood in us. Here we see the division between the inner and the outer cycle of the fundamental *heptaparaparshinokh*.

The process that goes on through the outer cycle of the heptaparaparshinokh continues through the planets and the moon and creates the whole physical world. There is also a creation that begins in the sun, where individuality enters, and leads first of all to the formation of tetartocosmoses or living beings, corresponding to World XLVIII. Then comes the possibility within the tetartocosmoses of the arising of intelligence or *Objective Reason*, which means the arising of three-brained beings.

Then it is said that the Creator gives his attention to certain of the three-brained beings so that they are endowed with the possibility of making an individual return to the Source. That is really the fourth creation. In it, we can speak of the fourth element in man, his own unity or "I" that does not come from his parents, the planetary conditions of his birth or even from the Sun, but straight from the Source, from God.[4]

The *tetartocosmos* is really an animal, and the microcosmoses are cells of the organism. When there is the possibility of a second body, then it is said that there are *beings*.

But the creation of intelligent beings has two forms. In one they are endowed with intelligence from the moment they are made. These are the "angels" described as arising on the planet *Modiktheo* from all three forces perfectly adjusted in the one act

---

[4]To those initiated into the language of triads, these correspond to four of the triads of order involved in conception:

3*-1*-2*	describes heredity
3-1*-2	describes planetary influences or fate
3-1-2*	describes solar influence or destiny
3-1-2	describes the gift of free will.

of conception: *martna*, *spirna* and *okina*. These naturally perfect beings are responsible for the government of the world and are closest to His Endlessness. But they are not able to meet all the situations that arise because they cannot fully enter into the hazards of the world. Therefore intelligent beings are needed who get to be intelligent the hard way.

The perfect three-brained beings of Modiktheo correspond to the Megalocosmos or World VI, which is beyond individuality. For all that, they are within the existing world and are therefore limited: a strain is set up between World VI, *megalocosmos*, and World III, Sun Absolute or *protocosmos*.

Gurdjieff wants to give us a shock by saying that a state of strain can exist at the highest level of the creation. It is not due to wrong action, but simply to the fact that between the finite and the infinite there is an incompatability that cannot be overcome. This is described in terms of radiations arising in the Sun Absolute from both the finite and infinite sources. The strain or predicament produced is called the *Choot-God-litanical period*. *Choot* is a Russian word meaning "almost" and *litany* means a supplication. Choot-God-litanical-period means: "when God almost had to ask for help."

The confronting of the finite and the infinite, or of the conditioned and the unconditioned produces an insoluble problem. There can only be approximate solutions. The planet Purgatory is such a solution.

In some way, the intelligences who return to the source must be enabled not to disturb the perfection of the source. Purgatory is in World XII where there is a special region or state of affairs in which the finite and the infinite meet. The strain or agony is transferred into World XII and World VI is "screened." It is not possible to pass through the screen until the limitations of existence are shed. This is what is taught in all religions, but it has become very distorted.

In the Christian religion, the original idea became so changed that it was taught that Purgatory was something that everybody is able to go through. Nowadays, people even expect to go to heaven without having to worry about Purgatory. In Islam, the teaching is that we have to go through a purifying suffering but eventually everyone will be brought to the paradise or Sun Absolute.[5] In Buddhism, the notion of *nirvana* is more explicit about the need to shed all craving for existence, all ill will and all separateness.

According to Gurdjieff's expression one cannot enter the Holy Planet Purgatory until one has overcome the egoism that makes one separate from other people. In the last but one chapter "Form and Sequence" Beelzebub explains to Hassein that written over the portal of the Holy Planet are the words: "Only-he-may-enter-here-who-puts-himself-in-the-position-of-the-other-results-of-my-labours." This means that it is necessary to have complete compassion.

Now, what is the Planet Purgatory? There was one very extraordinary book by St. Catherine of Genoa called *Purgatory* based on her visions. She saw that it was a state necessary to go through in order to come to the unlimited perfection. At the end of *Beelzebub's Tales*, Gurdjieff says that it is all nonsense that Paradise and Hell are other worlds existing somewhere or other and he says that they are "here beside us on Earth." The same planet can be Purgatory, can also be Paradise, can also be Hell or quite simply the animal fair.

We have the possibility of achieving liberation as Buddha says: "Here in this very life." Now the way of accelerated transformation is possible for many people. Everyone who comes to a certain stage of development enters into the stream that will eventually bring them to it. Gurdjieff says this many times in *Beelzebub's Tales*.

Everything, however, is to be taken literally as well as on a psychological level. Purgatory is a world and in that sense can be called a planet. It is the part of World XII in which one can see what is needed but because of one's defects is prevented from doing it. One cannot see this fully until the Master—the individuality—is fully awakened and present in us and there is a fully established relationship between the Master and the

---

[5]Remember, also, the comment of Gurdjieff to Mr. Bennett: "Paradise is easy, necessary go to Solei Absolu."

other parts in Worlds XXIV and XLVIII. This is described at the beginning of the chapter as everything outside being beautiful and ideal whereas inside is all the suffering. In that state, one is able to have everything of the lower worlds but one knows that one does not have the ultimate freedom, the deathlessness, until one is wiped out in one's separate existence. One is able to know what it is to go beyond existence altogether, which is described in the chapters as the Father Endlessness appearing to the souls on the Holy Planet Purgatory.

Why should our possibility of perfecting be so hard if everything is — as it is usually pictured — roses, roses in the higher world? Why should we be the only beings who can fail? Gurdjieff was very concerned that we should understand that everything is not roses, roses in the higher world. I remember once saying to him: "It must be the hardest thing of all to be God," and he looked at me and said: "It is so."

DISCUSSION

Editor's Note: Further explanations given by Mr. Bennett elucidated various questions that people ask about the chapter "Purgatory." Here, most of the questions are taken from those asked by students on the fifth Sherborne course which were recorded for the sake of this monograph.

Q. If the higher worlds are higher dimensional, why then is the Sun Absolute subject to the action of the Heropass?

J.G.B. In this chapter, the creation is presented as a series of successive steps, each one necessary to correct something missing in the previous step. This is inevitable as we cannot describe things or talk about them except in succession. If you were preparing a plan of a house, you would first of all have a general picture of the size and shape and position, how much accommodation and of what kind; then afterwards you would put in the details. But you might very well build the house in a different order. The way we build a house is totally different from the way this universe has come into existence. It is rightly said that this coming into existence is not subject to time in the way our actions are. The way we have of describing it is due to the way our minds work. It may be that the Creative Intelligence works in a totally different way. So many of the questions we can ask refer really to the way in which we have to talk about things.

Q. What is the difference between involution and evolution? Both presumably follow the law of seven: in one the energy being coarsened and in the other refined?

Q. How did the creation of the various worlds down to absolute nothing and the resulting reciprocal flow of energies produce a more stable situation to counteract the action of time? Isn't this just making a larger circle? There is something very significant here which I cannot grasp.

J.G.B. The change in the laws introduced the need for help from outside. The world has now to be such in which there is material for interaction. The emanations from the Sun Absolute result in there being other concentrations: second order and third order suns, eventually tetartocosmoses and so on. When this is set up, there is then a flow and counterflow, that is **involution** which is the going out from the Sun Absolute and **evolution** which is the return to the Sun Absolute. With that it is now possible for the wearing away of the Sun Absolute to be compensated. As the potential of the Sun Absolute diminishes it is renewed by feedback from the created world.

But in order to provide this feedback from the world, the flowing out has to continue. This gives rise to what is called in the chapter the **enlarging world**. The world is flowing out from the source, and so enlarges, to provide a means of return.

Not everything can return and there has to be a separation. From a substance of a given density one can obtain something of a finer quality at the expense of discarding something of a coarser quality. This is expressed in the alchemical phrase: "separate the fine from the coarse." We see this in our own bodies. Our bodies take in food with a certain potential and the process of metabolism or change is partly anabolic, upgrading, and partly catabolic, downgrading. The same principle is working throughout the whole world. It is possible for some parts to return to the source, but only because other parts will flow in the opposite direction. This does not mean that they do not return to the source, they do so but at the other end of material inertia. There is a separation of the more active and the less active. The more active goes through a process of purification until it is able to return to the active principle and the other goes through various stages of separation, providing nourishment at different points, until it returns and enters into the passive.[6]

Q. I think I get a feeling for what you are saying about the advantages of a semi-predictable world,[7] but what is the purpose of life here increasing its intelligence, what is the purpose of being able to accomplish all these variations?

J.G.B. The words "enlarging world" have to be taken into account here. It is in the nature of the second form of the laws that the world has to enlarge in order to provide feedback. The world is constructed in such a way that it is kept going by selection, by the separation of fine from coarse, and that is only possible if there is a supply to draw on.

As we know from ordinary experience, the larger things get the more unmanageable they get. Therefore one needs to put more and more intelligence into things. We can see intelligence running out in our human world.

You ask what is the purpose of it all. There is no pretence that we know what is beyond World VI. World III is incomprehensible. Why three forces? Why time and space? Why this kind of existence? To answer all these questions one has to get up to the beginning and ask whoever sits in World I. None of us has ever got there.

---

[6]See also The Boolmarshano of Makary Kronbernkzion in the chapter on "Man's Understanding of Justice."
[7]Nether chaotic nor wholly determined.

Q.   What am I personally to make of all this?

J.G.B.   The chapter Purgatory can be looked at as a psycho-logical allegory. We have to understand in our human lives that nothing is certain and predictable and that we have to bring intelligence to bear. We cannot attain stability of peace or immortality by the action of blind rules. What is said in this chapter can be taken to mean that we have to abandon the old teachings which say just obey the commandments and all will be well and come to something which is much more demand-ing; bringing our intelligence to bear just as our Endlessness brought intelligence to bear in order to renew His place of existence so we have to do the same in order to renew our place of existence — our planetary and higher bodies. In a way, what Gurdjieff says repeats the Christian doctrine that came particu-larly through St. Paul: the old law has only led you into sin and failure because you are unable to live up to it; it is not the fault of the law but man that you cannot live up to it; you are in hopeless trouble and there is no way out except through the entry of a higher law that takes uncertainty into account and depends on help from Above.

The failure of religion has brought about a great revolu-tion in our attitude towards the idea that if you only do what you are told then all will be well. It turns out that this does not work not only because we never do what we are told but because there are too many uncertainties. Even actions done with the best of intentions with strict obedience to the laws can produce disastrous results.

Q.   The alterations to the law of heptaparaparshinokh can hopefully be recognized in terms of our own experience. Are there any guidelines for such a search?[8]

J.G.B.   The possibility of taking a risk in order to achieve a gain is inherent in the modification of the laws. Because of the law of three it is possible to relate gain and loss in a special way.

---

[8]See also the section on the Law of Sevenfoldness.

This is the secret of triamazikamno and is expressed in the symbol of the enneagram which is only very indirectly referred to in *All and Everything*. The notion is that a combination of three octaves or three processes, if correctly adjusted according to the law of threefoldness, can achieve what one process alone cannot achieve. The question is how this adjustment is to be achieved. Here we come to the role of intelligence in the world.

Q. It's said that at the third order suns or planets the fifth stopinder is reached. Why does this give rise to "similarities to the already arisen" and in turn stops all further manifestations of the "outer cycle"?

J.G.B. It was necessary for the emanation of the Sun Absolute, the theomertmalogos, to go out from the Sun Absolute and participate in the creation of the subordinate cosmoses. There is a triad of the kind: reconciling-affirmative-receptive in which the initiating factor is the Holy Reconciling. The affirmative is a given newly formed sun and the receptive or denying the other cosmic concentrations which set up the constraints.[9] This triad sets up the order or structure of the cosmos that is coming. But it means that the Divine Intelligence is required to sustain the world. So we come to the next stage associated with the arising of "similarities to the already arisen" on the planets.

In the first emanation from the Sun Absolute there is a triad of involution: affirmative-receptive-reconciling in which the agents are theomertmalogos-etherokrilno-second order suns. The second order suns transmit the holy reconciling force and can therefore be creative sources in their turn. Then the third order suns or planets are subject to two different actions — one that comes from the prime source and another that comes from the secondary source. The result is that there is now a separation between inside and outside and it is said

[9]As in Ernst Mach's explanation of inertial mass as arising from the total universe of bodies.

that results are now partly inside, partly outside. What happens outside completes the "outer circle" of the fundamental cosmic *ansanbaluiazar*.

If we compare the worlds of will with Gurdjieff's terminology we have the following:

World I: Endlessness

World III: Protocosmos — Sun Absolute

World VI: Megalocosmos

World XII: Deuterocosmos — Second Order Suns

World XXIV: Tritocosmos — Third Order Suns or Planets

World XLVIII: Tetartocosmos

At the branching of the two creative streams there is the *microcosmos*[10] or living cell. The cell is the smallest cosmic unit that has its own independent existence. Below that there is no completeness.

Through the second grade cosmic law *Litsvrtsi* or the aggregation of the homogeneous *tetartocosmoses* arose from *microcosmoses*. It is then said that our Creator observed that certain tetartocosmoses had the possibility of independent locomotion on the surface of planets and he saw the possibility of them acquiring *Objective Reason*, that is intelligence. Special measures were taken to make this possible and these measures included the possibility of the forming in them of a second body. With that came the possibility of them having in them their own law of *triamazikamno*, that is, they could become three-brained beings. They were then no longer called tetartocosmoses but *beings* which implied that they were intelligences independent of the source.

This independent intelligence is characteristic of us men. That is why our place of existence is at the *harnel-aoot* of the universe, the most remote and difficult part of the universe.

---

[10]Bennett placed this between Worlds XXIV and XLVIII.

Q. I don't see the significance of the reproduction by three-brained beings on the planet Modiktheo.

J.G.B. It is possible to have intelligence already equipped with a higher being body and this is necessary on account of the second creative step. The universe is enlarging, there is an increasing complexity in the universe and there are required more intermediate intelligences for making the necessary adjustments.

This is all paralleled in the human body. It requires much more complex operations than the animal body and the moving instinctive centre is much more complex than that of animals. Our blood chemistry, nervous system and hormonal system are all elaborately adjusted in man within closer limits than with animals. There is more intelligence built into the human organism than there is in the animal organism.

Gurdjieff talks of the cells in the head brain which act as affirming forces. There is something equivalent to this in the *Megalocosmos* and the planet *Modiktheo* is put up as an allegorical representation of the formation of intelligences near to the prime source completely perfected from birth.

In the chapter on Justice, Gurdjieff very subtly puts it that intelligences near the source cannot really understand the problems of the world. He speaks of the researches of sacred individuals as missing the point because although wise "they were not direct". With all their perfect reason, the higher individuals are not able to enter into the sufferings and problems of the world in the same way as those who have acquired their higher bodies through labour and suffering. It is said somewhere that no one can enter into and understand the experiences of another who has not gone through them himself. This the perfected beings produced on the planet Modiktheo are not able to do.

We can go back to the early chapters of *Beelzebub's Tales* where sacred individuals who are concerned with regulating the process of the world fail to understand what it means to have sacrificed the potential of the human race in order to maintain the harmony of the solar system. It is a very powerful picture that is put in front of us here: a being of higher intelligence who is only concerned with maintaining the order of the universe can miss something that is frightful and it is only from Above that the necessary understanding and compassion can come. "Above" refers to the *Protocosmos* or Sun Absolute, whereas the beings of Modiktheo are in the Megalocosmos.

Q. Are these "higher being bodies" to be taken literally or are they just allegorical pictures or symbols?

J. G. B. They are to be taken literally. It is possible to exist in the higher bodies without this physical body.

The second or *Kesdjan* body is nourished by what Gurdjieff calls "air." That is why we do the *zikr* to provide food for our second body. This was the way used by the Masters of Wisdom, the *Khwajagan*, but there is something similar in other teachings.

The second body is of varying degrees of substantiality according to the degree of development or self-perfection that has been reached. In ordinary people, the second being body is no more than a ghost or shadow. It is only able to exist in the world of the psychic energies in its lowest levels. It is not very different from the material world. Once you understand this, you will see that what is called spiritualism only amounts to this. This state of existence is just one stage removed from the physical world and can really be called a dream replica or counterpart. The difference is that there are not the limits of the physical world. One will meet things in that world which are the thought forms of one's own life. It can be a very pleasant experience or a very terrifying experience. People attach a great deal of importance to it because they think it shows survival of bodily death, but what value it is they do not ask.

The second body of man can grow more robust until it is more substantial than the physical body and can have power over it. When it has that it can develop its own intelligence. Gurdjieff says more than once that real reason, real vision is only possible in the second body. The planetary body and the ordinary centres can only have relative reason or "reason of knowing."

The second body can give us the confidence that when we die we shall not be dreaming. In this chapter, it is said that if the required gradation of Objective Reason is reached during this life then the ultimate attainment of the Sun Absolute is assured, of returning to the source as an individual and not just as a part of the mass.

The Kesdjan body is not entirely free from time though its relationship to time is very different from that of the physical body and it can move through time and space, it can go into the past and future and do many things that the physical body cannot do.

It remains time-like in that events still happen in succession and is subject to the law of wearing out.

Rascooarno is simply derived from a Russian word meaning "separation of parts." The first rascooarno is the separation of the kesdjan body from the physical body. Then, it is said, the kesdjan rises to the sphere of existence corresponding to its own quality. For the sake of our eternal well-being it is necessary that we should see to it that our kesdjan body is brought to the point where it will be able to enter a sphere where its self-perfecting will continue. This continuing of self-perfecting means working out the consequences of life — what is called "karma." Whether this is done in life or somewhere else, something else remains when it is finished: the third part of man which is his will, his "I" or spirit. This is not material at all and is therefore indestructible. If it has formed its own body it is also able to act. Gurdjieff says very little about this and I will not go into it in more detail.

Q.   What is meant by the "Okipkhalevnian-exchange-of-the-lower-part-of-the-soul"?

J.G.B.   This would need a lot of time to explain. It is connected with the point we can come to in our second *rükü*[11] where

---

[11]Gesture of submission to the unity of all humankind and life.

we are all in contact with one another and it is possible for us to enter into one another. Thus it is possible for someone who has reached a certain stage of self-perfecting, but not reached the final liberation, to continue with the help of another by entering into that kesdjan body.

Q.   What we try to do about these bodies and so on, we do pretty much on faith that there is a good reason?

J.G.B.   On faith and on revelation; something is revealed to us about the higher world. The reason that we can discover a great deal is shown in the chapter Purgatory through the comic piece about God being pictured as an old Jew with a comb in his pocket. Gurdjieff says that the most important expression of reality that it is possible to make is to say that we are all "similitudes of the whole" and in man there are all the laws that govern the universe.

There is in the Qu'ran the saying: "He who knows himself knows his Lord." Because we are similitudes to the whole we are capable of knowing more than concerns our private affairs. As we see for ourselves that we must eat to live and nourish one another, we should be able to understand that this same principle applies to the world: that is, the *Trogoautoegocrat*.

Q.   Does conscience come in here? Is it anything to do with the question of why we should feel we have to make efforts?

J.G.B.   Yes, it is so. Conscience is the line of communication that we have with the higher. It is really the line of communication with the Cosmic Individuality.[12]

---

[12]Individuality of World III.

MERCILESS HEROPASS

T he chapter on the The Holy Planet Purgatory puts us in front of the fact that the world is not a perfectly ordered machine in which everything is going according to plan. If there is some kind of plan or purpose in the Creation then there is something that sets limits to the possibility of realizing it. Therefore there is a need for intelligence, sacrifice and labour and there is the possibility of failure.

Gurdjieff was at great pains to avoid the dualistic notion of good and evil. In the chapter on Man's Understanding of Justice he says that this is perhaps the most disastrous idea to have entered human thinking. He says that it arose in the time of Atlantis and was revived at the time of Babylon (sixth century B.C.).

A great deal of Gurdjieff's ideas, especially his cosmology, came from a very old tradition known in various forms, in particular in the Zoroastrian and in the Vedic traditions. In the Zoroastrian tradition there is a clear conflict of good and evil: Ahura Mazda, the good spirit and Ahriman, the destroyer or adversary who seeks to invade and devastate the creation of the good spirit. This doctrine was certainly adopted in Babylon and is what Gurdjieff refers to as the "Babylonian Dualism."

Side by side with the dualistic teaching was another called Zurvanism which said that there was an infinite reality beyond the good and evil spirits. In one of the texts that we have, there is a verse which even speaks of Ahura Mazda and Ahriman as twins. This is very difficult to accommodate in the orthodox teaching of good and evil but this verse seems to go back to Zoroaster himself.[13]

---

[13] *3rd Gatha, Yasna* 30, 3–5.

With the Sassanid Kings of Persia (A.D. 225–640) a form of Zurvanism flourished, firstly in the great cultural centre of Ctesiphon and then in Baghdad. It taught that there was an all powerful source of all, even described as the pitiless Zurvan. The good spirit creates a world that can be free from the destruction that necessarily follows the working of Zurvan. Because there is a conflict between the finite world and the infinite reality, the good spirit is limited in what he is able to do and this limitation permits the arising of the bad spirit or the adversary.

The purpose of this doctrine was certainly to get rid of dualism and try to return to the concept of a single source. It seems very likely that Gurdjieff took these ideas up in writing Beelzebub. The Merciless Heropass corresponds to Zurvan and the Creator Endlessness to Ahura Mazda or the good spirit.

There are various reasons why I believe that Gurdjieff derived his cosmological teaching from sources earlier than those which we know of in the written texts. One must understand that there were no actual written Zoroastrian texts until about the ninth century of the Christian era, that is, fourteen centuries after the life of Zoroaster himself. These texts were not written in the original language of Zoroaster's time but in an early form of Persian. It seems that Gurdjieff had access to an older tradition. It is possible that this is the Sarmán society which he mentions a number of times in *Beelzebub's Tales*[14] and also in *Meetings with Remarkable Men*. The Sarmán moved north (c. 324 B.C.) from Babylon to avoid the degeneration coming through Alexander of Macedon.[15]

---

[14]Bennett seems to be identifying the society *Akhaldan* with the *Sarman*. See also *Gurdjieff Making a New World* by J.G. Bennett (Wellingborough, England: Turnstone Press, 1973), pp. 68–9.

[15]See also *Meetings with Remarkable Men* by Gurdjieff, pp. 90–3. The havoc produced by Alexander is lamented in the later Zoroastrian texts such as the *Bundahisn* in terms almost exactly echoed by Gurdjieff in *All and Everything:* ". . .that archvainglorious Greek, Alexander of Macedon."

I believe that Gurdjieff got the idea of Heropass from the Sarmán. He uses Greek for this word because he intended its meaning to be accessible to anyone who would take a little trouble. In the same way, he uses colloquial Greek for the law of threefoldness, *triamazikamno*: "I put three together." He was equally familiar with Turkish, Armenian and Russian, and often uses a combination of words from different languages to coin a special term. In the word *Heropass* he is being quite straightforward and intends to tell us something by this word.

Hero means "holy one," but *pass* is the masculine form for "All." Heropass means, therefore: "The Holy One who is All" or "He who is Everything."

It may be that Heropass is a translation of the word Zurvan; and the word Zurvan in its turn is the same as the word Sarmán, for a change like that is easily possible in a transition from one dialect to another. Maybe the Zurvan society existing in Babylon was the same as the Sarmán society that Gurdjieff found in Central Asia.

If Gurdjieff had simply wanted to say Absolute Time, he would have used *pan* instead of *pass*: pan is the neutral term for "All." He makes the word Heropass which means that he intended it to be taken as a person. He speaks about the "merciless" and "pitiless" Heropass in exactly the same way as the old texts speak about Zurvan.

Zurvan is indifferent to the fate of the world. It is beyond concern with that, beyond concern with the success or failure of the creation. It merely establishes the conditions within which the creation is possible.

Zurvan or Heropass could be taken to mean just the Absolute, but there is more to it than that. Heropass is "that One who is the All-Holy." In Zoroastrianism, the Zurvanites were accused of worshipping Zurvan instead of Ahura Mazda, the good spirit. That is how it came to be rejected as a heresy, because in the worship of Zurvan one is worshipping the bad as well as the good. The Zurvanite heresy was preserved in certain sects such as the Yezidis. I visited the Yezidis myself and became convinced—though I could extract very little—that they have great knowledge.[16]

I must point out that we have been looking at the question of how this notion could have arisen for Gurdjieff and this is only, so to say, the historical aspect. Gurdjieff was brought up in a region where he came into contact with the Yezidis and Magians, just as he did with Christians, Muslims and Jews. But nowhere, for more than a thousand years, has the doctrine of Zurvan been openly taught. So we return to the notion that Gurdjieff made contact with the ancient society Sarmán in the region to which they migrated in the time of Alexander.

Now let us look at what Gurdjieff says about the Heropass. In the "Hymn to His Endlessness" in the chapter on "The Inevitable Results of Impartial Mentation" it is said that the Merciless Heropass is vanquished and the consequences of its working are neutralized. This idea also appears in certain of the old Zurvanite texts. It is, of course, never suggested that the conditions of creation are annihilated or that time ceases. What is said is that a certain state is preserved in which the lawful commands of the Merciless Heropass do not lead to destruction. This is not done by fighting against the commands but through the action of intelligence by which there can be feedback and renewal **within a limited region**. This points to the world as we know it, in which renewal is possible only through separation and not everything can be renewed. In the old tradition this is pictured as Ahriman being thrown out of the Creation and into the Absolute region.

The personal sense of the word Heropass or Zurvan seems to suggest that the Heropass "permits" the setting up of conditions in which our Father Endlessness is able to have a creation which is a good creation. For there to be a good creation, there must be a distinction for the word "good" implies that there is also something which is "not good." The dualism is secondary. It is only necessary because something has to be rejected. Evil is then not something fighting against good but that which has

---

[16]See also *Journeys in Islamic Countries* by J.G. Bennett, Vol. II, Chapter 6.

to be rejected in order to allow the good to fulfil itself. There is
something in these ideas that is very old and we can find in
nearly all the oldest Indo-European mythologies the idea of a
primal reality out of which came a creative spirit which has to
struggle. These mythologies — such as the Greek — are older
than the time of Zoroaster. There is therefore a very ancient
tradition which says that the good spirit becomes involved in
conflict because in order to create a good world there must be
separation. (I must add that Heropass cannot be taken simply
as a translation of Chronos. It does not fit nearly so well into
the Greek mythology as it does into the Zoroastrian.)

Gurdjieff also says quite simply that the Heropass is the
same as the flow of time. It is the inevitable growing old and
wearing out of all existing things. This reminds us of Buddhism
and Buddha's teaching on the nature of existence, *dukkha*.
There is no satisfaction, no permanence and no reality in it.
Reality is only in being liberated from existence. Common to
the notions of Zurvan, Dukkha and Heropass is the inevitabil-
ity of the dissolution of all created and existing things. But
there is one very important difference between two interpreta-
tions. In the one, the Buddhist, it is said that there is a possibility of escape from this world. One can find one's way into a
state of being where there is no longer dukkha: this is *Nirvana*,
liberation. In the other view it is said that it is possible through
understanding the laws to create a permanence by means of self
renewal. It is this view which prevails in *Beelzebub's Tales* and is
strongly stated in the chapter on Purgatory and on Impartial
Mentation. It is through knowledge of the laws and by making
use of the contingency and uncertainty of the world that one
can overcome the Merciless Heropass.

Amongst all the teachers and teachings I have made contact with and had respect for, there are great differences in the
way they present the overcoming of time. The Christian teaching is very peculiar in this way. It says that the Kingdom of
God is not of this world, it is a world we come to through death
and resurrection, a world of immortality and renewal. Yet it
also says that this world itself needs to be redeemed and transformed. The great central prayer of Christianity, the Lord's

Prayer, says: "Thy Kingdom come, thy will be done on earth as it is in heaven." It does not say: "Let us go to thy Kingdom" but: "Let thy Kingdom come here."

LAW OF SEVENFOLDNESS

n the Heptaparaparshinokh chapter it is said that every complete whole is made of seven independent elements, *tazaloorinono*, "the-seven-aspectness-of-every-whole-phenomenon." There is no reference to a sequence such as we find in the Purgatory chapter and the transition can be confusing. In Ouspensky's presentation of the law of seven in *In Search of the Miraculous* it appears entirely as a sequence making us think of a journey in which we go step-by-step. None of that is in the Heptaparaparshinokh chapter. The seven-tone musical scale or octave is no more described as a sequence than the seven colours of the spectrum or the seven components of opium. The observation is made that to fix a point in space and time needs seven independent parameters. Theophany's discovery of the law of sevenfoldness begins with noticing that the mixture of pine-resin and goat's milk crystallises into a form with seven definite plane surfaces.

The emphasis is on qualities and that is how we need to look at it: every complete process has seven different qualities in it and the happening of one thing after another is something secondary. The qualities on the whole appear in a certain order which is connected with the stages of the heptaparaparshinokh as described in Purgatory. But what is said in the two chapters is very different. One reason for this is that they do not come from the same tradition — or, rather, though they probably come from the same source it is by two different lines of transmission.

The two presentations need to be brought together, but this can only be done through our real experience. What is emphasised in the Heptaparaparshinokh chapter is the opera-

tion of different cosmic qualities. We need to have the taste of
the beginning, of committing ourselves to an action. If we do
not have it and we do not bring it into what we do then we can
never do anything; we are just carried along like machines.

Then there is contact. This is getting down to it, being in
it and doing what we are doing. It is the taste of that which
draws us out of the dream world.

Another taste is in the awareness of reciprocal action,
when the job that one is doing is responding. Something is
being shared. This is very clear in cooking when we feel that
the foodstuff is responding to us: it is changing from raw to
cooked; transforming. The artist is aware that the time comes
when the work of art is making a contribution of its own; it is
not all flowing **from** him **into** the work. In the Purgatory
chapter this kind of thing is given the name *tritoëhary*.

Then comes the birthpang of the process, the *harnel-aoot*
which is in the middle of the whole. There is the awareness that
something is missing. One is far from the beginning and far
from the end. In the production of a work of art there is a
moment where one feels hopeless. It is impossible to get any
further and yet one cannot go back and start again because too
much has happened. One feels that it cannot be finished, or if it
is that it will have nothing of what one looked to at the
beginning.

The fifth quality that we come to Gurdjieff calls *piandjoëhary*. People are often puzzled by what he says about this,
that it can give: "results not similar but opposite to each other."
Piandjoëhary corresponds to the moment of truth. There is an
easy way out, the path of compromise: when the energy of
piandjoëhary flows into us we can either enjoy it or serve it. At
this point we can make things easy for ourselves and it is very
tempting to do so. We have reached the point at which we have
already created something and only we ourselves can decide
what is to come of it. It is possible in this moment to give or to
take. We can be captured by what we are doing and at the same
time imagine that we are gaining and that we are the masters in
control. The reality is just the opposite: we are slaves. Only
when we leave ourselves out of it and serve the process can we

become masters. We become true masters by making ourselves slaves but when we try to become masters we become slaves. If we use our creative power for ourselves it destroys us. If we sacrifice ourselves in order to serve the creative power, then it creates us.

All of this can be seen in quite small things if we can recognize the different tastes, the different qualities. The usual — and cheapest — way of passing through the fifth stage is simply to take it easy. One is out of the time of trouble, the harnel-aoot, and one can do things one could not do before. One is in fact rendering it easy for oneself and it is very hard not to do this, especially in our work.

We have to be very very much on our guard when this moment comes. Things are going well and we are inclined to let them go well and not look for the extra perfection that is now possible because there is a power we did not have before. Many people lose their chance at that moment. In one of Gurdjieff's lectures he illustrated this by speaking of a young pupil whom he saw had very extraordinary clairvoyant powers and could be trained to know about the future and the hidden working of the cosmos. Gurdjieff worked with him to develop these powers. The time came when there was a lot of suffering and then things began to work for him. At that point, he walked away, became a professional, made money out of it and lost it all.

In Purgatory, Gurdjieff says the piandjoëhary is located in the cerebellum. It is described as a certain substance or energy and when it is awakened, naturally or artificially, the feeling comes that: "Now, I can do anything." When it is stimulated through drugs, people think they can fly and they jump out of windows.

On the whole, we are not very sensitive to this quality and therefore we tend to get into the way of compromising. When it is like that, we do not see what we are losing.

Then we come to the sixth component which is called *exioëhary*. In Purgatory, this is connected with sex and described as part of the transformation of the first being food. People often ask what is meant by the transmutation of the exioëhary and the use of it for feeding the higher being body. It must be understood that this is just one special illustration of the quality of the sixth stopinder. This quality is of going beyond itself. It calls for something in us that amounts to this: we have to **give** everything in order to go beyond. We come to the point where nothing can go further by being pushed from behind, as was the case in the previous two stages. What we have to do to cross the gap is to put ourselves in the position of the result. The result is called *Resulzarion*. Putting oneself in the position of the result means to put oneself aside and this requires more than being ready to serve the creative power.

It is a mistake to try and understand the law of heptapara-parshinokh from the outside. Heptaparaparshinokh is not something we can look at as an object of study, it is really something which looks out from us and experiences itself in us. That is why it is the taste that matters.

The taste of salt is something very different from anything we can know about salt. Nothing that can be said about a rose can give the smell of a rose. It is the same with heptapara-parshinokh. One has to go through it and experience it strongly enough, often enough, in large and small ways to find out what each of the *stopinders* taste like.

PART FOUR

WORK

WORK ON ONESELF

t is hardly necessary for me to remind the reader that the conception of the "nothing" which must become "something" is at the root of all religious teaching. It is the doctrine of rebirth, of death and resurrection which, however variously stated, has always the same content. Its whole significance and value is lost if its paradoxical character is attenuated. The sincere outburst "Thou fool, that which thou sowest is not quickened except it die"[1] is spoken from the heart of one who has seen in his own experience that it is meaningless to speak of rebirth without death. Gurdjieff speaks of this as "the death of that 'Tyrant' from whom proceeds our slavery in this life."[2] This is the all-important fruit of rightly conducted self-observation. I realise my own nothingness and in doing so, see that my life has been spent in slavery to a non-existent "Tyrant," that is, the imaginary "I" for whose hopes and fears and imaginations I have expended my energy. This is why the realisation of one's own nothingness is also called "the first liberation of man."

We have here the second decisive test which must be applied to any teaching. If it starts with the assumption that man already is, and offers to show him only how he can increase his own powers and his own value, it is necessarily and demonstrably false. Even if it teaches the necessity of rebirth, but does not show that before one can be born, one must first die, it does not possess the truth. Even if it teaches that one

---

[1] I Corinthians 15, 36.
[2] G.I. Gurdjieff, *All and Everything, Beelzebub's Tales to his Grandson* (New York: Dutton, 1973; and London: Routledge & Kegan Paul, 1950), p. 1232. Hereafter referred to as *All and Everything*.

must die but presents the idea as an emotional experience, a conscious renunciation of something one already has, it is deceptive and dangerous. That is why the phrase "realisation of one's own nothingness" is safer and more exact. But this realisation can only come from the ability to see objectively what it is to exist, and what it is not to exist. The knowledge of existence and the knowledge of non-existence are inseparable from one another, as are the knowledge of heat and cold, darkness and light. Until I can really distinguish and experience the two states—I know nothing objectively about either.

From this, we reach the third stage of "work upon oneself." The realisation of one's own nothingness is not despair. I do not mean by this that despair can ever be wholly absent even from rightly conducted work; but its arising and significance are quite different from the realisation of one's own nothingness. I shall refer to it later. First, it is necessary to come to grips with the question of what is meant by "work on oneself." For this, we must return to the concept of man as a three-brained being. I have referred to the three brains as being respectively the affirming, denying and reconciling forces in the triad of human experience. This idea can easily be misunderstood. To place the mind and the body in conflict as respectively the affirming and denying forces seems to lead simply to asceticism, that is, the subjugation of the body as an end in itself. Phrases such as "he began to labour consciously with a complete mercilessness towards his denying-part and to create intentionally disturbing conditions for this denying-part of his"[3] have all the appearance of advocating corporeal mortification of the kind typified in the Blessed Henry Suso of St. Peter of Alcantara.[4] Any such interpretation is contradicted by the insistence on the obligation to be just towards the planetary body, and "make demands on it only according to its inherent possibilities."[5] Any work which has undesirable consequences for the planetary body is not to be undertaken, however much we may like it and however

[3]*All and Everything*, p. 1131.
[4]St. Teresa, *Complete Works*, Vol. 1, tr. E.A. Peers, 1946, pp. 176, 194.
[5]*All and Everything*, p. 1172.

greatly it may interest us. But duty towards the planetary body is put even more specifically in "The Organization for Man's Existence Created by the Very Saintly Ashiata Shiemash" where the first obligolnian-striving for men is "to have in their ordinary being-existence everything satisfying and really necessary for their planetary body."

The apparent contradiction comes from a confusion between the sensing brain and the planetary body. The latter is described as "only a dependent cosmic formation, conscious of nothing."[6] It cannot take care of itself and it must therefore be treated justly so that it should serve the spiritualized parts properly.

The affirming and the denying-sources in man are "his head brain and the brain of his spinal marrow." In the ordinary conditions of mechanical life, these two brains function almost entirely out of contact with one another, and there is between them no relation of affirming and denying. When, however, a man begins to understand the process whereby matter is transformed in his organism for the formation of his higher being parts, he sees that a particular sequence of bodily states is required. For example, it may be necessary for his body during certain periods to remain in a certain posture to enable a particular process of the transformation and assimilation of energy to proceed. He knows this with his head brain, but the result has to be obtained through his sensing brain. He assumes the posture, but if he has learned to observe, he senses that it is full of imperfections. With his head brain, he demands more exactitude and greater concentration. However far his sensing brain may go in the required direction, it is not far enough; the concentration does not permeate his whole organism. His thinking brain says "I can," but his sensing brain says, "I cannot." **This is the affirmation and denial which constitutes the relationship of work upon oneself.**

The role of the feeling brain is to bring to bear the understanding which comes from past experience of success and fail-

---

[6]*All and Everything*, p. 1171.

ure. It is only when there is present in the feeling brain the realisation of my own nothingness, that is the experience of non-existence set over against existence, that the affirmation and denial of my thinking and sensing brains can be united into the single experience of "I can because I must." At first, it is by no means obvious that all work upon oneself resolves into this triad of the affirming, denying and reconciling forces in the thinking, sensing and feeling brains. Indeed this cannot be understood until a man has genuine experience of work upon himself. That is why it is impossible, or rather undesirable, to attempt to describe it. "Only he knows, who has tasted."

The creation of a new being in oneself is making something out of nothing. That is an impossibility, and it is indeed impossible. That is why despair must always enter into work upon oneself. For to despair is to realise that what I am seeking to do is impossible, and at the same time that it is necessary and that there is no escape from it.

CONSCIENCE

he legominism of Ashiata Shiemash is directed to the thesis that it is already too late to change the life of man by the "normal" ways based upon the impulses of Faith, Hope and Love. This emphasis is necessary because if this is not understood, the real "Terror of the Situation" cannot be grasped. Thousands of good people, anxious for the welfare of mankind, persist in the notion that these ways can and must be followed. Having rejected them, Ashiata Shiemash turns to the fourth Sacred Impulse, that of Objective Conscience, and concludes that through its regeneration alone can mankind be saved. The reason for this is subtle and needs explaining. In the first place, conscience itself is not understood, for it is often confused with morality. But morality is an externally imposed rule of conduct, whereas conscience is an independent self-judgment by which a being is able to determine, at any moment, what action to allow and what action to resist. No rules can be comprehensive or flexible enough to correspond to the complexity and variableness of human situations. Moreover, no rules can liberate man from the consequences of the properties of the organ Kundabuffer or provide him with a safeguard against his own egoism.

In the Legominism, conscience is taken for granted and the short explanation is given that it does not participate in the everyday life of man because the "abnormally established conditions of external ordinary being existence existing here have caused it to penetrate and become embedded in the subconsciousness and take no part whatever in the functioning of our ordinary consciousness."[7] He sets himself therefore the task

---

[7]*All and Everything*, p. 359.

of finding a means whereby the Sacred Impulse of Conscience can be made a permanent factor in man's ordinary waking experience.

In the description of Ashiata Shiemash's subsequent activities, it is explained that conscience emerges into the waking state only through conscious labour and intentional suffering. To induce men to undertake the effort and sacrifice, Ashiata Shiemash proclaims that "in the sub-consciousness of people, there are crystallised and are always present the data manifested from Above, for engendering in them the Divine Impulse of genuine Conscience, and that only he who acquires the 'ableness' that the action of these data participate in the functioning of that consciousness of theirs in which they pass their everyday existence, has in the objective sense the honest right to be called and really be a genuine son of OUR COMMON FATHER CREATOR of all that exists."[8]

Ouspensky describes a conversation in which Gurdjieff explains about conscience and the reason why it does not enter into the waking consciousness of man.[9]

"**Conscience** is a state in which a man **feels all at once** everything that he in general feels, or can feel. And as everyone has within him thousands of contradictory feelings which vary from a deeply hidden realisation of his own nothingness and fears of all kinds to the most stupid kind of self-conceit, self-confidence, self-satisfaction and self-praise, to feel all these **together** would not only be painful but literally unbearable. If a man whose inner world is composed of contradictions were suddenly to feel all these contradictions simultaneously within himself, if he were to feel all at once that he loves everything he hates, and hates everything he loves; that he lies when he tells the truth and that he tells the truth when he lies; and if he could feel the shame and horror of it all, this would be the state which is called 'conscience'."

In the same conversation, Gurdjieff goes on to describe how conscience is from early childhood removed from waking

---

[8]*All and Everything*, p. 368.
[9]*In Search of the Miraculous*, p. 155.

experience by deliberately inculcated pretence and self-deception. Conscience therefore remains asleep and "wakening is only possible for those who seek it and want it, for those who are ready to struggle with themselves and work on themselves for a very long time and very persistently in order to attain it."[10]

There follows a description of what is meant by conscious labour and intentional suffering. A man must "go out to meet all those inner sufferings which are connected with the sensations of contradiction. Moreover, the destruction of 'buffers' in itself requires very long work, and a man must agree to this work realising that the result of his work will be every possible discomfort and suffering from the awakening of his conscience." In this conversation, Gurdjieff draws the same distinction between conscience and morality as appears in the tales of Beelzebub. "Conscience is a general and a **permanent** phenomenon. Conscience is the same for all men, and conscience is possible only in the absence of buffers. From the point of view of understanding the different categories of man, we may say that there exists the conscience of a man in whom there are no contradictions. This conscience is not suffering; on the contrary it is joy of a totally new character which we are unable to understand. But even a momentary awakening of conscience in a man who has thousands of different I's is bound to involve suffering. And if these moments of conscience become longer, and if a man does not fear them, but on the contrary co-operates with them and tries to keep and prolong them, an element of very subtle joy, a foretaste of the future 'clear consciousness' will gradually enter into these moments."[11]

The submergence of conscience is ascribed in *Beelzebub's Tales* to the duality of the human psyche arising from the separation between the consciousness of the head brain and the consciousness of the feeling and sensing brains. This in turn

[10]*In Search of the Miraculous*, p. 156.
[11]*In Search of the Miraculous*, p. 156.

proceeds from faulty education which destroys the natural sincerity of children. "To teach and to suggest to their children how to be insincere with others and deceitful in everything, has become so ingrained in the beings of the planet Earth at the present time that it has even become their conception of their duty towards their children; and this kind of conduct towards their children they call by the famous word 'education'."

"They 'educate' their children never to be able and never to dare to do as the 'conscience' present in them instinctively directs, but only that which is prescribed in the manual of 'bon ton' usually drawn up there just by various candidates for 'Hasnamusses'."[12]

Hence it comes about that "The conscience which might be in the consciousness of the beings of that planet is, from their earliest infancy, gradually driven-back-within, so that by the time they are grown up, the conscience is already found only in what they call their subconsciousness." That is why the data for the arising of the sacred being impulse of conscience have escaped the degeneration to which all the other Sacred Being Impulses were subject, namely the impulses of Faith, Love and Hope.

[12]*All and Everything*, p. 378.

UNION WITH THE SOURCE

Beelzebub specifically states that the blending with that Greatness "must sooner or later be the lot of every already arisen essence."[13] This suggests a distinction between the essences which, "sooner or later," that is, as a result of an indefinite number of cycles of concentration and dispersion, are finally reunited with the whole, and those who, by discovering the way of conscious labour and intentional suffering, liberate themselves from the cycle at an earlier stage. Although, so far as I am aware, it is nowhere specifically stated, I think that this must be the meaning of the phrase "accelerated result" often used in *Beelzebub's Tales*. Beelzebub himself is addressed as an "anticipated accelerated result" in the final chapter which describes his apotheosis.[14] I think further that it is implied that it is only in an "accelerated result" that identity is preserved and appears finally as an "immortal cosmic individual."

From the second and third series of his writings, it is clear that Gurdjieff intends the doctrine of higher being bodies to be taken literally and with it the immortality of the soul. There is, however, the one all-important distinction from ordinary doctrines of immortality, namely that the soul is not present in man until it is acquired. Moreover he constantly reiterated that a soul is a rare and most precious possession, to which only those few can attain who are able and willing to pay the price.

We return then to the ordinary average man. What part has he to play in such a drama, where the strength of the hero

---

[13]*All and Everything*, p. 801.
[14]*All and Everything*, p. 1182.

and the single-mindedness of the saint are scarcely sufficient to overcome the difficulties of the long and perilous ascent and to reach the summit where alone eternal life is to be found? And here indeed the terrifying words, "For many are called but few are chosen" re-echo with a greater insistence by the very clarity of their interpretation. The perennial question arises as to the fate of the many. Are they, in the words of the Gospel, no more than "salt which has lost its savour, neither fit for the land nor yet for the dunghill"? There can be no doubt that Gurdjieff's "man" who "serves during the flow of the entire process of his existence exclusively only as a thing, which, when no longer needed, disappears forever," is precisely equivalent to the Gospel saying, "Every tree that bringeth not forth good fruit is hewn down and cast into the fire." Any mitigation of this inexorable sentence brings to nothing the significance of human life. Any view of human existence which denies or weakens the reality of the choice between life and death defrauds man of the very knowledge that can set him free. It is not by way of consoling and false hopes that the lot of the ordinary average man can be relieved.

It is not false hope but real hope that Gurdjieff offers. Salvation is not reserved for the rare religious genius and still less for the brilliant intellect. It does not depend upon the accident of birth or race or creed. It is not for the few because they are elect,[15] predestined for eternal life. It is for the few only because many fail to find the straight gate and narrow way. The seed of life — that is conscience — is sown in every man's heart and every man who seeks can find it. Throughout *Beelzebub's Tales*, the estrangement of man from his real destiny is depicted as an unnecessary avoidable tragedy. The organ Kundabuffer has been removed and man has been set free.

---

[15]Election is self-election; initiation, self-initiation. See also *In Search of the Miraculous*, p. 315.

SACRED ASKOKIN,
ABRUSTDONIS AND HELKDONIS

When we undertake something which is to bring order it requires effort and energy. This has to come from somewhere and something is transmitted to the task. To bring order deliberately, through an act of will, liberates conscious energy: when we undertake this, we give ourselves to the task and put ourselves under its demands. Part of the energy involved goes into the task. We can see that something has been achieved. What we do not see is that something has gone to serve a higher purpose.

In *Beelzebub's Tales* this is called "food for the moon" but there is no need to settle whether this is meant literally or not. What is sure is that man must produce something for the cosmic purpose. If he does this unconsciously — just by dying, for example — that is one thing. We have to serve the cosmic purpose "willynilly." It is another thing if man fulfils his obligation by conscious labour, by undertaking something for the benefit of the future.

In conscious labours energy goes into the visible result, but also food for the moon or *sacred askokin* is liberated which we do not see and really belongs to another sphere altogether. There is also something else. In the act of service there is the *sacred helkdonis*. HLK is a special root word that also appears in *Akhaldan*. The root signifies the creation, the cosmos, order. It is a conditioning in which it is possible to share things. In Sufi terminology, there is the *khalqa*, the circle of sharing in which there is a spiritual work. When we are together working to understand something, there is a khalqa.

Helkdonis comes as our own, as a direct action of our own being; Gurdjieff says that it is food for our higher being body,

but it is different from the *exioëhary* which is, so to say, there all
the time. It comes when we work not for ourselves but in order
to fulfil our cosmic obligation. Something returns into us. It is
not an energy or substance, it is really an action. If we can
grasp this, then it is possible to see that what this can bring is
something like a strengthening of our own will. But it is impossible to form a picture of this which is not a distortion.

We can look at it this way. Whenever we do conscious
work, the energy divides into three. One part is the energy that
goes into bringing about the visible result and this includes the
material energies involved. The second part is liberated for
some cosmic purpose. This is not like ordinary energy, it is
energy that can be used by higher powers.[16] The third part—
connected with helkdonis—is that in which we come closer to
our own source or to God. Something is added to our own
being.

When we do some conscious work—whether it is directed
outwardly or inwardly—what we see is just the visible result or
the experienced action. The sacred askokin represents the mystery of Work: that something of the merit of our own work is
transferred to the zone of a higher purpose. The words "transfer of merits" are used in religion to refer to the possibility of
someone's action making something come about in others. It is
this that makes it meaningful to pray for the dead, but it is a
very big thing to come to understand what that is about. The
third part at first glance looks as if it is just our own profit, like
a reward for having made an effort. This is how it is looked at
and spoken of: if we do something good we will get a reward.
But the reward is not like we think it is. The nearest we can get
to it is to speak of it as a purification. We become purer from
conscious service.

Editor's Note: There are more explicit passages on the
helkdonis—and also *abrustdonis*—in the early unpublished version of *Beelzebub's Tales*, in the chapter Purgatory. In that version, helkdonis is presented as the third food, the first being

---

[16]See also Chapter 35 of *The Dramatic Universe*, Vol. II, pp. 315-6.

ordinary nourishment and the second, air (including the finer substances originating in the planets and sun). The conscious assimilation of this food was a highly regarded task in Atlantis. It was called "helping God" and was recognized as "the chief thing for the improvement of beings in general." Ordinary nourishment gives "negative substances," air provides "positive substances" and the helkdonis the "neutralizing." Gurdjieff writes: ". . . these positive and negative substances become deified through the process of 'Helping God'."

In describing the transformation of food in the early version of the Purgatory chapter, Gurdjieff says that firstly abrustdonis and then helkdonis enter as neutralizing substances into the mixture arising from negative substances of the first food and positive substances already in beings. He goes on to say that the neutralizing substances arise in contemporary man from acute psychic experiences, voluntary or involuntary.

Later on, describing the emergence of exioëhary, i.e. sperm, he writes: "The forming and perfection of the *Kesdjan* is brought about by means of the substance called 'Helkdonis'." It is only this substance and abrustdonis that can take the evolution of the sex energy or exioëhary further. Abrustdonis is explained as the second food or "air." Through the evolution of the second food, air or abrustdonis, exioëhary is deposited and transmuted and gives rise to a second body, the body Kesdjan. When the Kesdjan is perfected, there begins to be deposited "owing to the sacred substances of the Helkdonis" substances formed from the emanations of the *defterocosmoses* (the second order suns). Towards the end of the chapter he adds that it is possible to meet and absorb those "residual substances which originated from the satisfaction of the Force of the Will of Our Prime Source, His Endlessness Himself."

Gurdjieff's final reference to helkdonis describes how struggle with the desires of the planetary body produces a friction which can form substances of the "divine Helkdonis."

In the chapter on War, abrustdonis, helkdonis and askokin are described as blended together. It is through the conscious assimilation of abrustdonis and helkdonis that askokin —

or food for the moon, the cosmic purpose — can be liberated in a way that does not require physical death.

Through air, neutralizing substances can enter "for the possibility of continuing their race." That is to say, the helkdonis is the third force in the conception of a new being. It is about this that Mr. Bennett commented in a talk on will-types January 10th, 1973.

The affirming and denying forces take place through the man and woman, but the third force, the Helkdonis, comes independently of them and this third force is what makes conception possible. Thousands of millions of sperm are involved in every sexual act and only a small number of sexual unions bring about a conception. A conception in the world of sperm is an exceedingly rare event. It is as rare as the appearance of a perfect individual in the world of men, one who is capable of going into the Divine World from this one. We may think this rarity to be unjust, but it is no more unjust than that vast numbers of sperm should perish for there to be one new conception. Both are exceptional events. Ordinarily we think that conception is just a matter of the accidental meeting of the ovum and sperm and that it is simply a matter of statistics. More is involved and if we artificially increase the probability of conception we do not increase the probability of a viable human being appearing.

We do have to make the distinction between a genuinely accidental birth and a birth that is a true formation of a human being. The latter is the rule. When this happens a type is created. The role of the helkdonis is that it brings in an individualized will pattern. This is the very core of the being but as it arrives from a different dimension or a different world it does not have a place in the material existence. We can say that it remains in the unconditioned world. A place has to be prepared for it. A great deal of our work consists in preparing a place for the entry of our true individuality that will remain in its own world until we have prepared a place for it here.

Although it does not participate in our life it does determine the possible form of our actions and more than anything the possible situations into which we can enter. The search for an understanding of types is very ancient. We have almost lost this in our times because we are conditioned to living in personality and we do not even feel the necessity of finding out who we really are.

Because of this, the world is full of misfits and very few people feel at home in their conditions of life.

In ancient times, there was a very persistent and even anguished search for this understanding. People were not subject to the heavy pressure of mechanization and had the awareness of the need to understand and also the leisure to do something about it.

Djartklom

Djartklom turns out to be one of the most important things for our Work. In *Beelzebub's Tales* it is referred to in at least three ways, each one of which is meant to convey something. Firstly, it is connected with night and day, darkness and light: this has to do with a very deep understanding of our consciousness. Secondly, it is connected with remorse of conscience — remorse being presented as a strong situation of djartklom. Thirdly, it is described as a dividing of the *Omnipresent Okidanokh* into its three constituent parts and their striving to reblend.

The third description is the key. It amounts to saying that an opportunity is created. The forces are separated — the affirmative, denying and reconciling — and in striving to reblend they produce an action in us. There is a possibility of doing something because of the separation of the third force.

The simplest case of djartklom, and one that is the foundation of all our possibilities of transformation, is the spontaneous waking up that occurs to us. We can be walking in the garden, lost in our associations, when something happens: our eyes are opened and we see the life around us. At that moment one nearly always feels a change in one's physical state. One feels that one has come into oneself and the plants and trees and animals which were not there suddenly are there.

How does this happen? It is not something we bring about. We were not even looking for it. We were lost and now we are not lost. Little by little we are learning to take these chances and make use of them. When they come we can work. When we are asleep we cannot work.

Everyone knows about this kind of change. Children have the experience of seeing and of changing over from not seeing to seeing; and they have the sense of wonder that accompanies such a change. Most people then become dull towards it. They become dull because they take such a moment as an opportunity for enjoyment and do not see that it is an opportunity for work. They feel it is enough to enjoy the beauty around them. But if one is really connected with Work, the moment arouses something else besides, a feeling that one does not want to be like one was a moment ago, one does not want to be living in a dream out of touch with the world and with oneself. When it is like that, it is an opening for us. That is what it is meant for.

Man is so constructed that his consciousness is subject to fluctuations. Sometimes he falls below normal to very low states, sometimes he rises above normal to very high states. That is how his possibilities come, but he has to learn how to make use of them.

A deeper djartklom is through conscience. Remorse of conscience comes without any action on our part and without having earned it. It produces in us the beginning of a deeper perception, like the "fear of the Lord" which is "the beginning of Wisdom."

Similarly, there are openings to the higher worlds that come to us during exercises or meditations which are not expected and where they come from one does not see.

To understand the special place that djartklom has in Gurdjieff's ideas, we must first of all grasp what *Beelzebub's Tales* is about. There is more than one way of interpreting this book. It can be looked at as a history of the spiritual life of man, as an exposition of real education and how to introduce people to the Work, as a series of parables and allegories in the tradition of Sufi teaching stories and as something prophetic dealing with the future of mankind. There is yet another way, that *Beelzebub's Tales* is Gurdjieff's own story. All the characters are different sides of Gurdjieff himself. This applies particularly to the stories connected with djartklom. He introduces two characters of the planet Saturn, Gornahoor Harharkh and his son Gornahoor Rakhoorkh. Harharkh appears very early on in the chapter "The Arch-Preposterous" with his wonderful apparatus for producing artificial djartklom. He is represented as a great scientist famous throughout the whole megalocosmos for his discoveries about the sacred okidanokh, or Will. He demonstrates the separation of forces to Beelzebub and produces the flash of blinding light of the reblending; but he never explains what it is all for. Towards the end of the book in the chapter on Electricity his son Rakhoorkh makes an appearance and it is said that Rakhoorkh's work has led to the discrediting of his father and even his disgrace. Gornahoor Rakhoorkh came to realize that his father's wonderful apparatus was producing the wrong kind of results.

I believe that Gornahoor Harharkh represents Gurdjieff when he was working at the Prieuré and that the wonderful apparatus for producing artificial djartklom represents the Prieuré itself. The clue is given by the phrase "artificial djartklom." The Gornahoor Harharkh way is **to act on people to wake them up**.

It was during the time of the Prieuré that Gurdjieff built up all his reputation for wanting to dominate over people and for the use of violent methods. His way of working changed afterwards. He changed from artificial to natural production of djartklom. The natural way is when it arises from within. **What the teacher has to do is to educate people to make use of the opportunities that arise spontaneously.**

Many people regard it as the role of a teacher to produce artificial djartklom. Some people even regard it as the central thing. I sometimes wish that Gurdjieff had not talked about it in *Beelzebub's Tales* in such a disguised way. There are very few people who have realized what is preposterous in the Arch-Preposterous. It would be very good if all people who set up as teachers put up a little sign in front of them: "Beware of Artificial Djartklom." The trouble is that it can produce spectacular results like Gornahoor Harharkh's blinding flash of light; but then everything returns to how it was before and even **something is damaged**. I watched Gurdjieff at the end of his life and even with all that experience I twice saw him make a mistake: two people went away from him and had a breakdown and eventually lost contact with the Work. But out of the hundreds of people that I saw him with in Paris he used artificial djartklom only a half-a-dozen times. At the Prieuré he had all sorts of elaborate conditions designed to cause frictions between people and he would constantly stir things up. Sometimes he would be ruthlessly cruel — not out of malice but simply to wake people up.

The point that Gurdjieff wants to make in *Beelzebub's Tales* is that there are two ways in which things can open for us. They can open from an action that is not from this world: not from ourselves, or from our inner self, nor from another person. This is because of the way the world is made. There is a "spiritualizing" action, an action that is not ours. The entry of this action into us I call the **seventh line of work**[17] and it is this that makes all the rest possible.

The action puts us in debt: we come under the obligation to do something. The second way is through the action of another person upon us and belongs to the **fifth line of work**.[18] There are times and places when it is necessary for this artificial djartklom to be produced.

A very good example of artificial djartklom is the stop exercise. If it works rightly for us, we have a moment when we instantaneously see ourselves, the quality of our thinking and the quality of our state. There is a separation between the part of our nature that is still and able to see and the part that is moving and cannot see for itself. Then the Work can enter. It is our understanding of that moment which decides what we will make of the opportunity.

If there is too much artificial djartklom, people come to depend on it. They come to the point when they cannot work unless somebody is doing this to them. I have seen people go to meetings to get bawled out and made to look stupid because they feel that by this they become more awake. It is quite

---

[17]See also Bennett's *The Sevenfold Work* (Ripon, England: Coombe Springs Press, 1975). The seven lines are: 1) assimilation, 2) struggle, 3) service, 4) manifestation, 5) receptivity, 6) submission and 7) grace.

[18]The moment of stop is in the fifth line, an action from outside. During the stop there is the second line; holding one's attention in oneself. After the stop is the third line; working consciously.

wrong. What happens in the end is that they actually come to need to be kicked around, otherwise they feel they are not working. It is probably also true that something gets really spoiled in the possibilities for natural djartklom.

I have said that we are under obligation in the moments of awakening. Take the example we began with of walking in the garden and coming to and being aware of the beauty around one. One must take the emotions that come to one — of wonder, of thankfulness, love of beauty — and bring out of them a strengthening of one's wish to work. When we used to listen to Gurdjieff playing the little hand organ, somehow he produced in me — and many others felt the same — a longing to purify myself, far stronger than anything I could summon up. I just wanted to be right, to be what I should be. Such things do not remain in one's consciousness. Something is distilled and enters into one's being: If one does not convert the experience of the rejoicing into a wish to be worthy of it then it is wasted. When one can ask: "Who am I to be allowed to enjoy this?" the djartklom begins to touch one's conscience.

We must try to understand what this kind of wish is like. In *Beelzebub's Tales* it is expressed as "non-desires predominating over desires."[19] This is a very difficult thing to understand as is the Buddhist teaching on the same subject. Most people believe that the Buddha taught that one should have no desires, but there is in fact no trace of this in the scriptures. What is meant here is that our wish for freedom must be stronger than our wish for things of this world. It should be more important to us to be worthy of enjoying than to enjoy; but this does not mean that one should not enjoy at all. What happens if one only enjoys is that it quickly slips into: "I'm better than other people. I have perceptions they don't have. I can tell them what wonderful things I have seen."

There is something further which needs to be said about djartklom. People believe that the "waking up" lasts for a period

---

[19]In the chapter "The Organization for man's existence created by the Very Saintly Ashiata Shiemash."

of time and they talk about it as if it had a duration. It is important to try and see that the moment of waking up is instantaneous and timeless. Afterwards, there are consequences. Maybe some energy is released and this keeps one in an enhanced state in which one is more aware — but this is not djartklom. Djartklom is like lightning: lightning is timeless but you go on seeing the flash for a very long time.

Finally, there is the picture Gurdjieff has given of djartklom in relation to night and day. People do experience what this is about but usually fail to recognize it for what it is. During a meditation, it can happen, as many people report, that there comes about some kind of absence. These moments of not being there can be divided into four kinds. Firstly, there is just getting lost in associations and this is quite ordinary. Secondly, there is falling asleep. Then there is the sharp break, the sharp discontinuity, but one comes back as if waking out of sleep yet knowing that it was not just ordinary sleep. Lastly, there is the genuine hiatus where one disappears and returns to exactly the same point not knowing if a minute or a second has elapsed. This is when our attention is exceptionally good. In the East it is known as *Samádhi* or trance. The Buddhistic scriptures speak of a timeless and spaceless experience coming after the four *dhyanas*[20] and what happens is that literally one goes out of time and space into another dimension, that I have called **eternity**. That is why it is impossible to tell how long the experience has lasted. And when one goes out of space and time one does not necessarily remain where one is. One can come to and find oneself somewhere else or in yesterday and one has the strange feeling that somehow one has got to get to today. Then one returns into oneself.

One can come out of samádhi at the same place and time, at another place and time, or from sleep.

The thing to realize about samádhi is that it is not induced by oneself. It is a kind of djartklom associated with "day" and "night." We should remember that in *Beelzebub's Tales* it is hinted

---

[20]See also *The Sevenfold Work*, pp. 106–7.

that the darkness is superior. In the early part of 1925, Gurdjieff was still very much influenced by the experience he had in July of the previous year when he really did die and returned to life. He tried to say something about these experiences in the chapters on "The relative understanding of Time," "The Arch-absurd;" and "The Arch-preposterous." It is not through our efforts that such things come to us.

In the deep state of samádhi there is not even blankness: **there is disappearance**. One has gone into the spiritual world called in Sufism the *álam-i imkán* and left behind the world of states of consciousness, the *álam-i arváh*. Then we are directly under the power of God and we become malleable. During such a time, the spiritual power is able to do something with us.

Being – Partkdolg – Duty –
Conscious Labour And Intentional
Suffering

The way foreordained by our Endless Creator for the perfection of three-brained beings is "conscious labours and intentional sufferings." This belongs to the spiritual reality and we cannot think about it in any ordinary way. Unless we can see something beyond this world *being-partkdolg duty* cannot mean anything to us. It is about going beyond this world into some different kind of action. There is a great working in the Universe — is this just the working of a machine? If it is not a mechanical working then what is it? It is no use bringing in ideas of angels or beings of a special kind. What are such beings supposed to contribute to the action of the world? If it is mechanical do special beings make a difference, do they stop it being a machine?

The important things we need to understand are accessible if we just turn towards them. There is this air. What is it? It is endless: no inside or outside, no boundaries of its own and no surface. Left to itself, the air and every particle of air moves freely. In any moment countless millions of particles from our atmosphere spread throughout the whole solar system and countless millions of particles coming from all parts of the solar system enter our atmosphere. However attenuated it becomes the quality of the air remains, even in spaces where it is a million million times rarer than the air we breathe.

All life breathes and all breathe the same air. Air is the support of life or a medium of life. It is the medium of sound and of the water vapour that is needed for the nourishment of life. Without air, water could not come to the land and without air we could not bear the radiation of the sun. The air separates the bearable from the unbearable; it takes the unbearable into itself and lets us have the beneficent qualities. Through air, water and sunlight the barren rocks become the fertile soil that supports life, but air is the medium of them all.

Air gives us a picture of limitless generosity, giving itself freely to all. Everything — large and small, necessary or destructive, good or bad — is given the same air to breathe. Air can be for us a representation of the limitless compassion by which everything is supported. In reality, air is that compassion; it has the qualities we ascribe to it not by virtue of our thinking but in a way far more concrete than we can imagine.

We are surrounded by spiritual qualities, but they do not belong to beings and certainly not to us people. They are part of the working that sustains this life.

Gurdjieff uses the words "conscious labor." What kind of labour can be called conscious and what is it to make efforts consciously? Everything that lives has to exert itself. A plant has to thrust its roots down into the ground and thrust its leaves up into the air. Everything has to work in order to live. This is not conscious work, it is a necessity of functioning at all. All that lives has got to fulfil that minimum requirement and so have we.

Looking at ourselves we can also see that there are things we are driven to do by our own nature. Some of this is a genuine kind of work, doing something to fulfil ourselves, essence-work. Some of it is imaginary, resulting from suggestion, something that is picked up from the social environment. This can amount to slave-labour and always there is an element of slavery in it.

There is striving after some goal or other, after some reward. We can work very hard to achieve something and such efforts are, of course, legitimate. Nearly everyone enters the psychokinetic stream through some striving after a reward: becoming better, stronger, free from this or that trouble, attaining higher levels of being and so on. None of that belongs to conscious labour. Conscious labours must always come under the requirement of **acting without regard to the fruits of action**.

There is work simply and only because one must work. A mother serves her child because she must. If she does it for the sake of some reward she is terribly misguided. However hard the work of the mother is, however much she might complain, the work has to be done and it is not **for** anything.

It can be put as plainly as this: whenever we see something that must be done it means that we become conscious. Seeing what is necessary and seeing what is necessary, as necessary, is the first condition of conscious labour. It is only when we do what has to be done simply because it has to be done that work can liberate us from our own egoism. If we work for a reward, this reward is bound to be connected with the satisfaction of something in us and almost certainly this something will include our own egoism, self-love.

The difference between this kind of work, conscious work, and what is imposed on us because we have to live and maintain ourselves, is not something one is aware of instinctively. It is something one is aware of because of one's human nature.[21]

Gurdjieff always presents the idea of conscious labour as connected with **service to the future**, as the sower sows the seed in hope but unconcerned with who will reap the harvest. In *Beelzebub's Tales* all those who reach objective reason through conscious labour and intentional suffering are people who serve the future of mankind. This connection with the future is intrinsic to what conscious labour is; it is not just a matter of emphasis, taking for granted ordinary ideas of service in the present situation. Conscious labour is preparing a better future.

The sower is followed by the reaper who in his turn is preparing the future. The grain is not to be consumed in the harvest field; it is to be stored and converted into flour and later made into bread. At every step the fruits of action are to be enjoyed in the future. Why must this be so? It is because the future is the realm of creation; it is open to be created while the present is closing up, perishing, coming to an end. The closer we come to the present moment of time the more this perishing is inevitable.

---

[21]Which is partly spiritual, that is, *unconditioned*.

Every significant thing that has come into this world has taken time to give its fruit and for the greatest things, hundreds even thousands of years, have been required.

The serving of the future is a very special action and a way of liberation from the falsity and blindness that Gurdjieff described as "consequences of the organ Kundabuffer." From Kundabuffer comes grasping, demanding for ourselves, avoiding reality, deceiving ourselves and others, and all those things that are only possible so long as we live a false, pretending life. If one sets oneself to serve the future the pretending must give way, but what is there to give support? Here we come to **intentional suffering**. Without this, conscious labour will run into dryness and become empty.

We have to be clear in our minds about the different kinds of suffering. There is a kind of suffering that is harmful, which we can call "evil suffering." It is harmful in its origin and harmful in its results. All the suffering that comes from ill-will, hatred and rejection of others, is of this kind.

The second evil suffering is doubt and this is not so easy to understand. Doubt is the condition where one is asking for evidence and proof and refuses to accept anything unless it is shown. Where does this come from? It comes from one's own egoism and the wish to have something without having earned it. We need to grasp that this doubt is a sin.

In this world the next step in front of us is always clear and we can always tell at the very moment what we have to do. When it comes to tomorrow there may be questions and uncertainties, but if we say: "How can I go on unless I am given some assurance about tomorrow?" we are making an illegitimate demand. Many people suffer from this kind of inner questioning and agonising. On the surface it can appear to be justified but it is both a self-indulgence and a manifestation of egoism. When we see doubt is a wrong kind of suffering then our attitude changes. We see that it is not necessary to have certainty. There is a difference between asking questions and demanding answers. We can live perfectly well knowing what is to be done at this moment without any certainty as to the outcome or as to what will happen tomorrow.

The third evil suffering is grasping. From this many forms of suffering arise: fear of privation, fear of loss, all the suffering that comes from possessiveness in our personal relations with one another over external things. All that has to do with demandingness, concern with mine and my rights, produces a suffering that is illegitimate.

The fourth is self love which in its most obvious form is self pity. There is a whole range of suffering that comes when we have too much concern for ourselves. Very much suffering comes because we will not accept to suffer and people who will not take the unavoidable suffering pile ten times more suffering on themselves.

Finally there is the suffering connected with time, such as impotence and regret. We suffer because of something that happened in the past or because something does not happen that we are expecting or hoping for. Pak Subuh put it this way: "You are suffering because you are trying to go faster than God."

All these kinds of suffering are illegitimate. It may be they are what sin really consists of. The evil suffering is more serious than self indulgence because through self indulgence there can come a certain freedom from one's own egoism.

The evil suffering roots egoism more firmly in us and it was towards this that Gurdjieff directed his injunction: "You must learn to sacrifice suffering." Then there is suffering which is not so much sinful as futile: worrying, indignation about injustice, anxiety about the future. None of this does any good to anyone. It is *vikarmic*[22] suffering. This also we must learn how to sacrifice. It does not necessarily come from a wrong place in us but it is unnecessary and for some people results in a kind of paralysis.

Besides these, there is suffering that is genuinely unavoidable, such as the suffering that comes from disease, humiliation and bereavement. This is not illegitimate; it has to come in

---

[22] *Vikarma* is usually translated as "harmful action." It would be better to use the word *akarmic*, meaning "useless."

some form and all of us have to have it. It is suffering that is
capable of being transformed and this distinguishes it from the
harmful and useless kinds which are incapable of being transformed into a positive result. Unavoidable suffering can even
be a means of purifying our spiritual nature.

By way of illustration we can turn to the story of Ahmad
Rafai, the founder of the Rafai dervish order. He led a very
hard life in which he was rejected because of unorthodoxy in
his interpretation of Islam. He also undertook very severe
ascetic practices. He said: "I wanted to get into the Kingdom of
Heaven and I tried one gate after another but there were
always so many people trying to get in that I couldn't get
through the crowd. And then I came to one gate where there
was nobody and I got in very easily and that was by the gate of
humiliation." If one knows how to profit by humiliation it is
wonderfully easy.

Suffering due to illness can very easily become a matter of
self pity and graspingness. People can exploit illness and then it
is a very big loss for them. The real suffering when one is close
to death is different from that. Whoever has been near to death
in sickness knows that a door is open. Things have happened to
me that could only have happened when I was close to death.
There is nothing one can be more thankful for. Very often I
have been with people suffering from cancer. It is very strange.
Not only the person suffers but all those around who care also.
I have seen many many times that in this disease there is not
only the destruction of the body but also a curing of the soul.
There is something in the suffering that comes with failure,
humiliation, disease, the approach of death, bereavement
which is capable of being transformed into the positive or
sacred feelings. Out of them hope and faith can come, obedience can come and love can and does come. I remember a man
incapable of love who with his family was in terrible tension
and even hatred. In dying of cancer, he became a peaceful and
happy man reconciled with all his family. Another I knew had
the most terrible vices, after having become suddenly rich. His
life had a terrible ending in terms of suffering, yet through this
he was able to finish with all the bad things in his life.

There is a period of remission in this strange disease when it is possible to either forget what has been revealed or to hold on to it, as if it were a test to see what people themselves then do.

The particular kind of suffering cannot be sought for nor should it be. It opens a particular door to people and they can learn how to go through that door. There are not many people crowding round the door marked cancer.

It is wrong to believe that the suffering that I have called unavoidable comes to us as a punishment for our sins. One must understand that punishment for sin is a privilege. (For myself, I have always prayed and asked: "Let the consequences of my actions come quickly upon me.") The suffering that comes can be the opening of a door; it can be an opportunity given to someone to set themselves free. This is totally different from punishment in the sense of retribution. Gurdjieff makes clear in the *Lentrohamsanin* chapter[23] that his belief is that retribution is an exceedingly rare situation. The suffering that comes from the working of higher laws is a means opening to us, a way of freedom.

In all the cases up until now, the suffering involved has come to us or arisen in us without our own action taking part — it has happened to us in some way or other. When it comes to suffering in which we take an active role, Gurdjieff distinguishes between **voluntary** and **intentional** kinds. Voluntary suffering is quite straightforward. It is suffering one imposes on oneself to achieve something. The typical example is that of the athlete who disciplines himself, submits to the orders of the trainer and deprives himself of most of the natural pleasures of life in order to win a race. Another characteristic example is that of the miser who goes without things, even starves himself simply in order to accumulate money. Such suffering is connected with labour that is directed towards some reward or other. It is only justified by its fruits. To some extent it can take us beyond the result we aim at, but not very far.

---

[23]"The Destruction of the Labours of the Saintly Ashiata Shiemash."

Now, what is meant by intentional suffering? This is the crux of it all. Intentional suffering is the suffering incurred, that one exposes oneself to, in order to do one's duty. In doing one's duty one has to accept a situation which may, not necessarily will, result in trouble for oneself. The simplest example is doing something for the benefit of someone and being quite prepared to accept the ingratitude and misunderstanding that may result and make one's relationship with that person worse than if one had passed by on the other side.

The great Messengers demonstrate very clearly how it is. Let us begin with the example of Buddha. At first he followed the path of voluntary suffering. With five companions he set himself to conquer his own nature by means of severe asceticism. It was the way of the athlete. After a time, he saw for himself that this was not leading to freedom and that through this way one must remain in bondage. He went and looked behind it all until finally he saw what was at the root of human slavery and he became free.

Then came the temptation of Mara. Mara said to him: "You have attained enlightenment. You are now free, you have no need to remain in this world, you can go into the perfect freedom." When one has seen what this life is and how great a thing it is to go beyond the limitations of existence one can know what a temptation that really is; but Buddha replied: "No, I've an obligation to manifest. I have to share all this." Mara tries to persuade him that he will fail and that people will not understand but Buddha rejects him. Buddha took on himself the task of sharing what he had seen with others. During the next fifty years he lived a very hard life of constant labour. His own son turned against him and there was a split in his following because some people thought his way was too lax and a stricter discipline was needed. He was rejected by the Brahmins who did not like his discarding of the privileges of caste. So it went on. At the end of his life as an old man walking from village to village, town to town, to help the people who were in need, he came to his last meal with Chunda, a smith. The Buddha said: "Give me the truffles and give the rice and cakes to the others." He then went and buried the truffles. That is how it had to be.

The whole of the Buddha's life after enlightenment is a picture of what is meant by conscious labour and intentional suffering. The suffering was not imposed on him. He freely accepted the obligation to prepare something for the future of mankind and through that the suffering came. But this does not mean that the Buddha was an unhappy, miserable creature. On the contrary, there is every indication that he was joyful and humorous while his life was one of labour and suffering.

Muhammed, the Holy Prophet of God, also followed a path of intentional suffering. He was first of all a very successful young man known as "Muhammed the trustworthy." Then the spiritual power brought him to Mount Hera where it was revealed to him that he had to proclaim the unity of God. He was terrified. It was quite clear to him that he would be rejected. His wife Khadija and two others alone supported him, while the whole of Mecca turned against him, at that time the centre of pilgrimage for the Arab polytheistic religion. He was exiled and went to Ethiopia. He lost everything and wandered, constantly rejected and constantly misunderstood. Only in the last years of his life, from sixty to sixty-three years of age, does his life appear to be good. Even then, one must not forget that his only son died—that is a very hard thing—and there had been many hardships and illnesses. At the very beginning, Muhammed saw clearly that what he had to do would get him into trouble. It is then intentional suffering.

I need hardly speak of the example of our Lord Jesus Christ. The whole picture presented to us in the Gospels is of a man of sorrows well acquainted with grief. He never ceased in his labours, wandering from village to village, accepted and rejected, until the final sacrifice. All this was seen in advance and was intended.

It is never different with the perfected man. Gurdjieff in his own way exemplified the same principle of conscious labour and intentional suffering for the sake of the future. Whenever there is a need of something for the sake of the future there is a need for people who are able to bear the stresses that will come with change; and there has to be preparation. This is represented in the life of Jesus whose mission did not begin until he was over thirty years old. The same is true of the Buddha and Muhammed did not begin his work until he was nearly forty.

Is it that conscious labour and intentional suffering is only for the special rare ones or their disciples, followers, companions or apostles?

It is different in these times. The needs of the world are very much wider and there is a task that can no longer be performed by a few. Many people are needed. Jesus said that the harvest is plentiful but the reapers are few and now it is even more so like that. The harvest is enormous — the whole future of mankind.

"How is it to be with us?" It is not enough to say: "I wish to serve. I must be able to serve." It is not legitimate to say: "I'll serve when it suits me," because it works out that we have to serve just when it does not suit us. "Watch and pray for ye know not the day nor the hour when the Son of man cometh." We have to be like the air and let everything take us, deny ourselves to nothing, let everything be transmitted through us.

DISCUSSION

Q. I can say in my mind: "I really want to commit myself in this way" but it is very superficial. How can it be made deeper? I don't get hold of, I don't see the things that need to be done. So much escapes.

J. G. B. We all have this. You must look at it as a whole. How often have I said: "If only I had noticed that, I would have done something about it" when it is too late. Now I see that I have to accept it. There are certain kinds of defect that do not seem to change. On the other hand there has come a greater all-round awareness of the Work. It is more rooted in me **as a whole**.

When one sees an obstacle in oneself in the way you describe it can be converted into a stronger desire to work on oneself. It is really a particular kind of involuntary suffering and it can be transformed. When things go wrong, particularly when this is due to something in ourselves, the energy that comes from the failure can be directed into our Work.

There is a parable about this in the *Mathnawi* of Jalál ad-din Rumi. It is probably an old story that Rumi was retelling. A man goes to the mosque for prayer and as he arrives he meets the people coming away. One of these people asked him: "Where are you going?" "To pray," he replies. "You are too late," he is told: "The Prophet has already given the final benediction." At this the man utters a cry: "Ah!" The other looks at him and says: "You give me that 'Ah!' and I will gladly give you my prayers."

Awareness of our own negligence can be a very great source of energy for us in work. To try and overcome it directly may not be effective; I cannot tell.

Q. It seems to me that the higher intentions of intentional suffering can very easily become contaminated. How is one to deal with this?

J.G.B. One part of the answer is that we can help one another. By all accounts, Muhammed would never have undertaken his mission if it had not been for his wife Khadija and for his uncle who supported him when he was full of doubts about himself and the vision he had had. He was tempted to give up because it seemed to him a terrible presumption that he should believe he had received a direct command from God. In that kind of temptation, where one is frightened that the voice of God may be the voice of one's own egoism, one needs to turn to others.

It is also terrible easy for ill-will to enter into it. When someone has a sense of mission he can very easily feel that those who oppose and obstruct him are evil and he will think ill of them. The really pure ones never fall into that trap.

Q.   Christ said that those who are not against us are for us. But what of those who are against us? What attitude should we have towards them?

J.G.B.   In the Sermon on the Mount, Christ said: "Resist not evil." It is full of things like that. If a man takes your cloak let him have your coat also; if he makes you go a mile go with him twain; bless them that curse you, pray for them that despitefully use you and persecute you.

Q.   The idea of intentional suffering seems easy enough, but the real application of this to things in life is very difficult. That is when all the doubt arises.

J.G.B.   You must understand that this suffering is not something to be run after. This is put very clearly in the Gospels describing the scene at the Mount of Olives. "If this cup may not pass from me except I drink it, Thy Will be done." There was no running after it. It is made perfectly clear that there was no other way for what had to be done, then all that followed. When Ananda, the Buddha's favourite disciple, was in despair over the imminent death of Gotama, the Buddha called him back from the monastery where he had locked himself away and had him brought back into this life and his duties. There are many stories like that which show that intentional suffering is a matter of accepting the suffering that comes with a task that has to be done.

Q.   In what you have said there is something very true, very substantial. It had a profound effect. But now it all begins to recede when I think of the prospect of doing something in the world. How are we to conduct ourselves. What are the difficulties? What sort of attitude should we have?

J.G.B.   If you come into this Work only for what you can get for yourself, you will be disappointed. But something else can enter, the realization that it does not matter what one can get for oneself as long as one can do something that is necessary. That is a real step in our transformation.

Q. Can you say something more about how this whole thing of service can be kept pure without confusions and doubts and selfwill and the rest of them getting in the way?

J.G.B. What is needed is understanding. You may accept what I say. You even have had some moment when you really had this attitude towards suffering. As yet, it is not your own. It is not yet established in you what has to be eliminated, what transmuted, what accepted. There is no short cut to it, but it will come.

This understanding of suffering does not make us perfect but it is a great thing not to see suffering as an affliction. For that the inner eye must open which can see things as they really are. You come to see the working and you see that suffering is required; and you no more want to avoid it than you want to avoid putting your next foot on the ground when you are walking. In the spiritual path, joy and suffering follow one another like the two feet and you come to a point of not minding which "foot" is on the ground. You realize on the contrary that it is extremely uncomfortable hopping all the time on the joy foot.

CATACLYSM NOT ACCORDING TO LAW

he time of the Tiklianishian civilization (Sumerian) more or less corresponds to the dynastic period in Egypt. It was a time of the division of man into castes and the appearance of a middle class. It was then Gurdjieff says that mankind was divided into two streams owing to a "cataclysm not according to law." In the one stream, men are carried into the boundless ocean from which it is possible to rise to higher states of being by the action of "cyclones." In the other stream, men pass tumultuously through rough places and finally seep into the crevices of the earth to take part in the recycling of life. What decides whether a man is in one or the other stream is whether or not he has his own "I" by the time of reaching responsible age.

What is the catastrophic event? There has come about a fundamental misconception of the significance of human life. Something goes wrong for people before they reach responsible age. Gurdjieff is not talking about egoism but about something that we do to our children.

People believe in this material world as the reality and barely believe at all in a spiritual world. We hardly realize what this means. We hardly see how mad that is. Because of it people consider what they see and touch to be the reality and what they cannot see and touch to be unimportant. Children are brought up in such a way that what matters is how they **appear** to others and not what they really are. So people put their trust in the visible world which is perishable and not in the invisible which is imperishable. This Gurdjieff describes elsewhere as "seeing reality in one's attention reflected upside down" — so that "a fly becomes an elephant and an elephant a fly."

Can we accept this extreme statement that amounts to saying that human life is shattered by education and is the reason why people lose their souls? Education directs all our attention towards knowledge and attaches no importance to understanding. Exposing children to this kind of influence means that they reach adult life having lost themselves, being entirely dependent upon external things—possessions, the opinions of other people, appearances and so on—in other words, with no "I."

It is important to grasp how it is that seeing the spiritual world as a reflection of the material one means that we cannot have "I." "I" is not in the visible self yet this is what is suggested to children. Can there be a return to customs in which children are not persuaded to pretend things in order to get noticed?

In looking at the picture of the two streams, we can see that Gurdjieff intends to convey that there is something certain and assured about the path of men who have "I"; but the image of a "smooth flow through broad valleys" is a weakness in the presentation. We need to look at the social consequences of the majority reaching responsible age without their own "I."

Gurdjieff describes the general psychosis to which man is subject,[1] and he also refers to the adaptations produced by Great Nature "for the equilibrium" such as changes in the birth rate and the "tempo of the general psyche." Then he comes on to the critical social consequence: "the life of mankind . . . as every sane-thinking man ought to constate can now flow more or less tolerably only if people are divided into masters and slaves." Why should this be so? Why should it be a consequence of mankind dividing into the two streams?

If we contrast the life of a man with "I" with that of one without an "I" we must not confuse this with some idea of a perfected being. Having one's own "I" is the **beginning**. If one has an "I" this does mean that life will flow in a certain way but it does not mean that such a person is going to act rightly in

---

[1]G.I. Gurdjieff, *All and Everything, Beelzebub's Tales to his Grandson* (New York: Dutton, 1973; and London: Routledge & Kegan Paul, 1950), p. 1234–5.

everything. There is no guarantee against eogism and there remain differences between people that have to be taken into account.

Having one's own "I" links up with what is said in the chapter "The Organization for men's existence created by the Very Saintly Ashiata Shiemash." In particular, there is a clue in the fifth *obligonian striving* — to help each other reach the stage of self-individuality, *martfotai*, of the man who is really **Mister**.

What one has to get hold of is that simply by everybody "being themselves" there is no solution to the problem of collective human existence. Maybe this is obscured, as I said before, by the image of the broad valleys and uninterrupted flow that Gurdjieff presents.

We are trying to see how the sort of society we are living in at the present time has come about and what it entails. The story begins about 5,000 years ago at the time of the rising of the city-states which had far larger groupings of people than had previously existed. At that time there arose commerce and the first monetary systems. The invention of money had the result of fixing people's attention on visible, measurable values so that things began to be valued not directly in terms of their use to us but in terms of some token. It seems a sensible thing to do but it took attention away from the direct needs of human life. Before, when there had been exchange of goods, everything was in tangible form related to what was needed for the support of life. Now a step was taken away from life and there began to be fixed in people the belief that there were values existing outside of them which were to be measured in terms of wealth of money and acquisitions.

People became specialized. As a consequence, state organizations and governmental systems arose, taking people's attention further and further away from life. According to Gurdjieff's intuition and what he learnt from old traditions, before this time there was no stratified, social structure and no division into castes. We do not know, there is hardly any evidence about the social life of people before 3,000 B.C.

In the period that followed we can see the priests converting spiritual values into material terms as if they were convert-

ible into cash just like food, knives or pottery. Such is the
general historical picture.

This does not explain Gurdjieff's conclusion on the need
for there to be masters and slaves. He even says: "Although to
be either masters or slaves in a collective existence among
children, like ourselves, of the COMMON FATHER, is
unworthy of man . . . we must be reconciled to it . . . ." One has
to make oneself look at this collective existence and how men
can be towards each other when they do not have their "I."

Men without "I" have a void that will be filled by dominating or by being dependent. If someone tells you what to do
and how to be, there is an illusory security; being a slave
satisfies the thirst for security. Being a master is a substitute
for having an "I", the emptiness is covered up by manipulat-
ing others. Masters and slaves are really in the same
predicament.

In my own scheme of society I have described people who
are not concerned with the realization of their being as *psychostatic*. There are two forces at work in such people: dominance
or dependence. These are the two ways of escaping from the
emptiness that is within when there is no "I"; they are the two
refuges of egoism. This results in four combinations: the
entirely dominant ones I called *leaders*, that is *masters*, the
entirely dependent ones I called simple *dependants*; those who
express dominance not over people but over materials in creative activity, the *artists* and *craftsmen*; and those who express
their dependence by productive work and service, the *pro-
ducers*. Now we must take this question further. In any society
we can picture there must be a division of roles and different
people playing different roles. There must be the strong and
the weak and this will affect what people can do and how they
relate to each other. In the ordinary way of life dependence is
always slavery: how is it to come about that the strong can
help the weak and avoid the relation of subordination and
dominance?

The trouble is the strong cannot help the weak without
dominating. Historically we see this time and time again: domination in the name of good, providing help. The Dutch in the

East Indies were very benevolent and brought a high level of order and prosperity; yet it was a world of dominance and dependence. The Dutch could never understand why they were resented. This pattern has been repeated time and time again. Something is missing in the idea that a good society can arise from the strong helping the weak.

Beelzebub's Tales is very carefully written and all the necessary clues are put in. There is not trickery and nothing is misleading. The important clue he gives is in the passage I quoted above: "children of a common Father." This says something about "I" which we should try to understand. **There is no difference in "I" between one person and another**. One "I" cannot be master of another as they are all particles of the same God and God cannot be greater in one place and lesser in another. If you really understand about "I" you will see that there cannot be a relationship of domination and subordination between one "I" and another. When people recognize each other in this way, there is no feeling that one is better or worse, more or less important or privileged. The "I" is not to do with higher and lower. The "I" in man is his will. This will is his own individual will and unique. It is entirely himself. At the same time it is also God.

God is not something different and separate from us, another Will outside. He is not separate and yet each one of us is independent and free. Those who have their own "I" therefore neither feel themselves better nor worse, neither superior nor inferior, to others. They have no need either to impose themselves or to depend on others to give them an assurance that "they are."

Yet in terms of manifestation in this world some have one role to play, others another role. The society which is free of "masters" and "slaves" is not one in which everybody does the same thing — tills his own field, builds his own house, bakes his own bread and lives his own unique and enclosed life. On the contrary it is a fully articulated society in which everyone plays his own role. The point is that there is full independence of the person and his role. This goes all the way, even to the gifts of the spirit. As St. Paul said, the gifts are different but the spirit is the same. This has always failed to get over because we have got conditioned to look at life in terms of what is visible and tangible. What Gurdjieff is talking about in these passages is the inability of people to recognize the sameness of "I" in all of us. In that resides the equality, the fraternity and so on which were the slogans of the French revolution. These slogans are only real for people who have their own "I." If we look at men in terms of "I" we are all free, equal, brothers and sisters.

If only we could see our roles as temporary, like masks we put on and take off. In the relationship of master and slave, the master identifies with his role and plays that role because he believes he has a right to. It is different when you play a role simply because it is your turn to do so, or because you happen to be there to fill that place.

It is very good when there is a situation in which the roles are changing and not fixed. There is little doubt in my mind that we need to be able to change from the role of teacher to that of pupil, and from that of pupil to teacher. By fulfilling the role as well as possible and not being identified we can find our own "I". As long as one is identified with one's role, the role takes the place of the "I" and becomes a false "I." We substitute our egoism and self-centredness for our individuality. The individuality is totally non-egoistic because it is not centred in ourselves and it has no centre.

This is the truth expressed in the *rüküs*. First we turn to our own individuality, then to the realization that there is a will we share with others and then to realizing that it all comes from one source and one will that unites us all. The will has the, from the ordinary point of view, incomprehensible property that it can be unique and individual in each being and at the same time one; not only in the sense that it is one in the source, in God, but that it is also one in a society.

It is possible, at least for a time, for a number of people to have a single will. The secret of the unity of will is the unity of vision. The unity of vision permits the wills to recognize one another and then they become like one will. Then we can work together without authority.[2]

Gurdjieff speaks about being "children of a common Father." It is a very important saying and one of the important sayings in the Christian faith. What does it mean that something of The Father has entered into all of us? The Father is very different from a Creator who makes things outside of himself. The Father, God, has entered into us. If it were not so then the word "father" would mean nothing. Because God is not divisible, it means that the whole of God enters into us. That is the essential mystery which we just have to accept. Our minds cannot grasp that we can be at one and the same time unique individuals with unique individual wills and also be sharers in the collective will of human society or life and even the will of the Source of everything existing, the will of God.

If this mystery is explained in some logical way it gets distorted — either man has free will in which case he is independent of God's will or God's will is in everything, in which case man is wholly dependent on God — and we come back to the illusion of dependence and dominance. It is very unfortunate that we have the word "Almighty" because we start suggesting to ourselves that God somehow dominates over us and our will is something dependent. This is quite wrong, but it is very difficult to become aware and see that it is wrong. What is not so difficult is to come to recognize and respect the individuality of others and to be free of the need for dominance or dependence. If we do not see this in people we are still looking at them through the eyes of the organ Kundabuffer.

The idea that we are all children of a common Father was an enormous step which took mankind from belief in the special hemitheandric men to the belief that God is in **everyone**.

---

[2]Bennett is referring to the experiments he initiated at Sherborne, England, under the title "Special Projects" in which people came together in practical work starting from a common vision of the work to be done. These experiments have continued and proved astonishingly effective. People find their own place and no one is told what to do.

This new belief came out in all the faiths of the last 2,500 years. We are now at a time when a new step has to be made. But the situation of division into two streams will remain for a very long time, perhaps for twelve thousand years.[3]

We have to realize that passing from one stream to the other is to pass from the psychostatic to the psychokinetic order of society. The psychokinetic stream is the one destined to enter the boundless ocean, which represents psychoteleios man. But the possession of one's own "I" does not suffice for the reversal of the way of looking at life **that is needed for the sake of society**: to be free of dependence and dominance, free from dependence on external things or the need to have possessions or power. What really matters is to see that the "I" in one man is equal to the "I" in every other man.

At the end of *Beelzebub's Tales*, Gurdjieff is saying that, given the situation that we are all suffering from the consequences of the "cataclysm not according to law," and given that this cannot be changed within our lifetime — perhaps not for a very, very long time — some kind of compromise has to be found. This is that we should learn to play the role of masters with the sense that we do not do so by right. If I play the role of teaching you this does not mean that I am superior to you and that I am entitled to fill this place because I am something and you are not. If I thought such things it would mean that I would be falling back into the state of the cataclysm and judging by external things — that I am older and know things that you do not know. Owing to the cataclysm, the deepest truth about mankind has been twisted and distorted. The division of people into superior and inferior is a cataclysm not according to law. How many of us understand?

---

[3]That is half a Great Cycle of 25,000 years. This is the time needed to produce a change in the very nature of man. See also *Masters of Wisdom* by J.G. Bennett.

FRAGMENTS

ook for how Gurdjieff puts in something which at first you might not notice but which is the real sting in the tail. One should be able to bring these images out and see for oneself; they are like lenses which bring something into focus. You should not be satisfied in knowing only the first order presentation.

Remorse of conscience is seeing that something in us is preventing the ruler from ruling. Remorse is connected with *okidanokh*, will.

Concerning the assimilation of the higher being foods: *cognized intention* (pp. 569, 781-3) is knowing what one is doing; intentional absorption (p. 783) is knowing why one is doing it. These are connected with *contemplation*.

In "Form and Sequence" contemplation is differently expressed from how it is in the *Third Series*. Every day we have intense experiences. Within twenty-four hours we should contemplate that experience in the light of another of similar intensity. If we find ourselves awakening in the middle of the night, then it is the time to contemplate ourselves.

In "From the Author" Gurdjieff picks up the thread where other teachings leave off—such as the Buddhist teaching of no "I."[4] There is no exaggeration in the stories of the "free men" and the other descriptions.

---

[4]This is, of course, only a cursory statement of the Buddhist scheme which cannot be pinned down by a single phrase.

Regarding the five strivings of Ashiata Shiemash, the notion of "self-perfection in the sense of being" may be misleading. This does not refer to perfection in the sense that one always does the right thing and so on. There is no such being. There cannot be owing to the limitations of existence. Our faults are still there, but our illusions fall away (faná — as represented in the Great Prayer). There is no perfected being who lives in the world of "the lions laying down with the lambs." The secret is in connecting what Gurdjieff says about Conscience in Ashiata, with the Third Series: the title *Life is Real Only Then, when "I am"* says it. A being may be **free from illusions** — that does not mean that he does not make mistakes. "The real man has inside him his own law of three" — in this sense man is made in the image of God, in this sense he contains all the characteristics of the Megalocosmos. We must rouse the denying force, then struggle with it — it is holy. Between the positive and the negative reconciliation comes.

I would like to tell you of a discovery I accidentally made a few days ago when I was reading a book that I happened to pick up on the Zoroastrian sacred literature of the 9th century A.D.[5]

In this book there was a chapter on the word *farrah* which comes from the word *hvareno* in Zend. It is connected with Gurdjieff's word *Tzvarnoharno* which he put in the *"Hearld of Coming Good."*

The author of the book traced the history of the word *hvareno*, which is often taken to mean the "majesty" or the halo that surrounds the king or the great man. In the later history of the word it entered into different languages and in Armenian it became *park*.[6] Obviously, this is the word that was chosen by

---

[5]H.W. Bailey, *Zoroastrian Problems in the Ninth-Century Books* (Oxford: Clarendon Press, 1971).

[6]The source word was *farnah* in Old Persian and *xvarenah* in Avestan. It has derivations in many languages in many forms. Bailey says that the "word *farrah* belongs to the heroic age vocabulary. . .the ancient heroes carried out their feats by means of farrah" (ibid, p. xvii). The original word developed into the Christian Greek *doxa*, glory, and the root *par* in Armenian produced *p'aranor*, felicity. In the East, Sogdian developed the root *prn* and in the

Gurdjieff to put into the expression *being-partk-dolg-duty*, which means: what is intrinsically right of itself. Being-partk-dolg-duty is that which brings a complete welfare, spiritual and material, together. It means that which can assure us of the complete welfare of the individual, of the society and of mankind.

Before I came across *Beelzebub's Tales*, which was only in 1948 as before that we had been forbidden to read them by Ouspensky, I had expressed this notion in the word *psychokinetic*.

Buddhist texts it "is used of the four stages of the Buddhist way of life." In the old Avestan language the word contains the root *ar*, to work. This appears again in the later Zoroastrian Pahlavi language in roots such as *ark* and *arg* and in the derivative *argastan*, "work," with the second component *stan* as in *datasan*, decision. Bailey traces it through very many languages, showing how it turns up in old Indian in the noun *rbhu*, artificer, in Slavonic Greek and, of course, Armenian, the loan-word *arbaneak*, "worker," *arbanekem*, "to serve."

EPILOGUE

n the 20th October, 1949, I went to Paris. I had telephoned for news of Gurdjieff, and was told that he was completely exhausted and staying in his room. My taxi from the airport took me through the Rue des Acacias and I stopped to ask one of his many pensioners for news. As I turned, I saw Gurdjieff standing before the fruit stall at his favourite greengrocers and when I reached him he was ordering a huge bunch of bananas "pour les anglais." It was one of his jokes that the English had no bananas, and every English visitor must be given two at each meal.

I walked back with him to his café at the corner of the Rue des Acacias and the Avenue MacMahon. He had not been out of doors for a week and an endless stream of French beggars, and aged Russian and Armenian exiles came up to his table for alms. Invalids — a young man paralytic — a woman evidently near despair — approached him. A few quiet words of advice — some medicine — or instructions to a doctor — and they left with an air of encouragement and fresh hope. Someone came in and paid him a large sum of money as a thank offering for a cured paralysis. It was soon distributed among the beggars. Children came for sweets, old friends of the quartier to say a word of greeting. All rejoicing in the belief that he would now get strong again — none suspecting that they were seeing him for the last time.

The last weeks of Gurdjieff's life were like that. It was as though he had decided to leave not a single loose end, nothing untidy behind him. Indeed in the weeks that followed his death, we became aware with growing astonishment of the meticulous care with which he had provided for everything.